PORTRAITS AND DOCUMENTS

SIXTEENTH CENTURY

Edited by

J. S. MILLWARD

Senior History Master
Bristol Grammar School

HUTCHINSON EDUCATIONAL

HUTCHINSON EDUCATIONAL LTD

178–202 Great Portland Street, London, W.1

London Melbourne Sydney
Auckland Bombay Toronto
Johannesburg New York

★

First published 1961

*This book has been set in Fournier type face. It has
been printed in Great Britain by The Anchor Press,
Ltd., in Tiptree, Essex, on Antique Wove paper
and bound by Taylor Garnett Evans & Co., Ltd.,
in Watford, Herts*

Contents

ECONOMIC AND SOCIAL

Illustrations

ACKNOWLEDGEMENTS

Acknowledgement is gladly made to the following for permission to use copyright material:

The Royal Historical Society for extracts from the *Camden Series*; the Hakluyt Society for a passage from *New Light on Drake*; the Early English Text Society for part of Bishop Fisher's sermon on Henry VII; the Clarendon Press for extracts from Prothero, *Statutes and Constitutional Documents* and Greville's *Life of Sir Philip Sydney*; the Cambridge University Press for excerpts from *A Discourse of the Common Weal of this Realm of England*, edited by the late Elizabeth Lamond; the Yorkshire Archaeological Society for extracts from their Record Series III; the Essex Record Office and Mr A. C. Edwards for passages taken from his book, *English History from Essex Sources*; Messrs Longmans, Green & Co. for an extract from *John Gerard: the Autobiography of an Elizabethan* by Philip Caraman; Messrs. John Lane the Bodley Head for material from *The Fugger Newsletters*, Second Series; Messrs Blackwell & Mott for an extract from More's *Utopia* translated by G. C. Richards.

Unpublished Crown Copyright material in the Public Record Office is printed by permission of the Controller of H.M. Stationery Office.

Every effort has been made to trace the owners of copyright material. The editor apologizes for any omissions, and would be grateful to know of them so that acknowledgement may be made in any future editions.

Introduction

Since I believe that first-hand material is of supreme importance to the teaching of history, there seems little need to justify the appearance of a collection of documents and illustrations. My attempt has been to remedy two perennial difficulties: how to obtain access to contemporary material and how to make copies of it available to all pupils for study. Obviously the choice of such material must be personal; there are also omissions from this volume because suitable documents or illustrations could not be found. Some of those which do appear in this collection may seem hackneyed, but often this is because they are still the best choice, and in any case will not be stale to those for whom they are intended, who will probably be seeing them for the first time.

Because of the limits of space, the documents chosen illustrate English history; those relating purely to Scotland and Ireland have been omitted. Comment and footnotes have been kept to the barest minimum in order not to trespass on ground that is the prerogative of the individual teacher, and to encourage the pupils to ask questions and think for themselves. Spelling has been modernized throughout to provide uniformity and to obviate the difficulties which can be seen in the examples with original spelling in the Appendix.

I would like to thank Professor R. B. Wernham for his helpful advice, my colleague Peter Arnold-Craft for constant constructive criticism and suggestion, the publishers for their kindness and patience, and Miss Ann Howgate for her invaluable help in many ways and especially with the illustrations. My debt to my wife is beyond acknowledgement.

J. S. M.

PORTRAITS

Henry VII

Source: the funeral sermon preached by Bishop Fisher at St Paul's, 10 May 1509. *The English Works of John Fisher* (Early Eng. Text Soc.) i. p. 269

Plate 2 and Appendix

His politic wisdom in governance it was singular, his wit always quick and ready, his reason pithy and substantial, his memory fresh and holding, his experience notable, his counsels fortunate and taken by wise deliberation, his speech gracious in diverse languages, his person goodly and amiable, his natural complexion of the purest mixture, his eyes fair and in good number, leagues and confederacies he had with all Christian princes, his mighty power was dreaded everywhere, not only within his realm but without also, his people were to him in as humble subjection as ever they were to king, his land many a day in peace and tranquillity, his prosperity in battle against his enemies was marvellous, his dealing in time of perils and dangers was cold and sober with great hardiness. If any treason were conspired against him it came out wonderfully, his treasure and riches incomparable, his buildings most goodly and after the newest cast all of pleasure. But what is all this now unto him, all be but *fumus & umbra*. A smoke that soon vanisheth, and a shadow soon passing away.

❖

Henry VIII

It should be noted that this was written when Henry was a young man, whereas most of his portraits were painted in middle age or later.

Source: despatch of Giustiniani, the Venetian Ambassador, *Cal. S. P. Venetian*, ii. p. 559

Plates 3 (a) and (b)

His Majesty is twenty-nine years old and extremely handsome. Nature could not have done more for him. He is much handsomer than any other sovereign in Christendom; a great deal handsomer than the King of France; very fair and his whole frame admirably proportioned. On hearing that Francis I wore a beard, he allowed his own to grow, and as it is reddish, he has now a beard that looks like gold. He is very accomplished, a good musician, composes well, is a most capital horseman, a fine jouster, speaks good French, Latin, and Spanish, is very religious, hears three masses daily when he hunts, and sometimes five on other days. He hears the office every day in the Queen's chamber, that is to say, vesper and compline. He is very fond of hunting, and never takes his diversion without tiring eight or ten horses, which he causes to be stationed beforehand along the line of country he means to take, and when one is tired he mounts another, and before he gets home they are all exhausted. He is extremely fond of tennis, at which game it is the prettiest thing in the world to see him play, his fair skin glowing through a shirt of the finest texture.

Cardinal Wolsey

Source: Giustiniani, *Despatches*, ii. p. 314

Plate 4 (a)

This Cardinal is the person who rules both the King and the entire kingdom. On the ambassador's first arrival in England he used to say to him, 'His Majesty will do so and so': subsequently, by degrees, he went forgetting himself, and commenced saying, 'We shall do so and so': at this present he has reached such a pitch that he says, 'I shall do so and so'.

He is about forty-six years old, very handsome, learned, extremely eloquent, of vast ability, and indefatigable. He, alone, transacts the same business as that which occupies all the magistracies, offices, and councils of Venice, both civil and criminal; and all state affairs, likewise are managed by him, let their nature be what it may.

He is pensive, and has the reputation of being extremely just: he favours the people exceedingly, and especially the poor; hearing their suits, and seeking to despatch them instantly: he also makes the lawyers plead *gratis* for all paupers.

He is in very great repute—seven times more so than if he were Pope. He has a very fine palace, where one traverses eight rooms before reaching his audience chamber, and they are all hung with tapestry, which is changed once a week. He always has a sideboard of plate worth 25,000 ducats, wherever he may be; and his silver is estimated at 150,000 ducats. In his own chamber there is always a cupboard with vessels to the amount of 30,000 ducats, this being customary with the English nobility.

He is supposed to be very rich indeed, in money, plate, and household stuff.

The archbishopric of York yields him about 14,000 ducats; the bishopric of Bath 8,000. One-third of the fees derived from the great seal are his; the other two are divided between the King and the

Chancellor. The Cardinal's share amounts to about 5,000 ducats. By the new year's gifts, which he receives in like manner as the King, he makes some 15,000 ducats.

❖

Sir Thomas More

Source: A letter from Erasmus to Ulrich von Hutten, dated Antwerp, 23 July 1519. *Epistles of Erasmus* (ed. F. M. Nichols, 1901) iii. 388

Plate 5

To begin with that side of More of which you know nothing, in height and stature he is not tall, nor again noticeably short, but there is such symmetry in all his limbs as leaves nothing to be desired here. He has a fair skin, his complexion glowing rather than pale, though far from ruddy, but for a very faint rosiness shining through. His hair is of a darkish blond, or if you will, a lightish brown, his beard scanty, his eyes bluish grey, with flecks here and there. . . . His expression corresponds to his character, always shewing a pleasant and friendly gaiety, and rather set in a smiling look; and, to speak honestly, better suited to merriment than to seriousness and solemnity, though far removed from silliness and buffoonery. His right shoulder seems a little higher than the left, particularly when he is walking: this is not natural to him but due to force of habit, like many of the little habits which we pick up. There is nothing to strike one in the rest of his body; only his hands are somewhat clumsy, but only when compared with the rest of his appearance. He has always from a boy been very careless of everything to do with personal adornment, to the point of not greatly caring for those things which according to Ovid's teaching should be the sole care of men. One can tell even now, from his appearance in maturity, how handsome he must have been as a young man; although when

I first knew him he was not more than three and twenty years old, for he is now barely forty.

His health is not so much robust as satisfactory, but equal to all tasks becoming an honourable citizen, subject to no, or at least very few, diseases: there is every prospect of his living long, as he has a father of great age—but a wondrously fresh and green old age. . . . His voice is neither strong nor at all weak, but easily audible, by no means soft or melodious, but the voice of a clear speaker: for he seems to have no natural gift for vocal music, although he delights in every kind of music. His speech is wonderfully clear and distinct, with no trace of haste or hesitation.

He likes to dress simply, and does not wear silk or purple or gold chains, excepting where it would not be decent not to wear them. . . .

In social intercourse he is of so rare a courtesy and charm of manners that there is no man so melancholy that he does not gladden, no subject so forbidding that he does not dispel the tedium of it. From his boyhood he has loved joking, so that he might seem born for this, but in his jokes he has never descended to buffoonery, and has never loved the biting jest. . . .

In human relations he looks for pleasure in everything he comes across, even in the gravest matters. If he has to do with intelligent and educated men, he takes pleasure in their brilliance; if with the ignorant and foolish, he enjoys their folly. He is not put out by perfect fools, and suits himself with marvellous dexterity to all men's feelings. For women generally, even for his wife, he has nothing but jests and merriment. . . .

He diligently cultivates true piety, while being remote from all superstitious observance. He has set hours in which he offers to God not the customary prayers but prayers from the heart. With his friends he talks of the life of the world to come so that one sees that he speaks sincerely and not without firm hope. Such is More even in the Court. And then there are those who think that Christians are to be found only in monasteries!

❖

Thomas Cromwell

Source: Eustace Chapuys, the Imperial Ambassador, to Nicolas de Granvelle, 15 Nov. 1535. *Cal. S.P. Spanish* 1534–5. p. 568

Plate 4 (b)

As you desire me to give you a detailed account of secretary Cromwell and his origin, I will tell you that he is the son of a poor blacksmith, who lived and is buried at a small village distant one league and a half from this city [London]. His uncle, the father of a cousin of his, whom he has since considerably enriched, was cook to the last Archbishop of Canterbury [Warham]. In his youth Cromwell was rather illconditioned and wild. After being some time in prison he went to Flanders, Rome, and other places in Italy where he made some stay. On his return to England he married the daughter of a fuller, and for a time kept servants in his house who worked for him at that handicraft. Later on he became a solicitor, and thereby became known to the late Cardinal of York [Wolsey] who took him into his service. At his master's fall he behaved very well towards him; and on the Cardinal's death, Master Wallop, now ambassador at the Court of France, somehow threatened and insulted him; whereupon, to save himself, he [Cromwell] asked and obtained an audience from King Henry, whom he addressed in such flattering terms and eloquent language—promising to make him the richest King in the world—that the King at once took him into his service, and made him councillor, though his appointment was kept secret for more than four months. Since then he has been constantly rising in power, so much so that he has now more influence with his master than the Cardinal ever had; for in the latter's time there were Compton, the Duke of Suffolk, and others, to whose advice the King occasionally listened, whereas nowadays everything is done at his bidding. The Chancellor [Audley] is but a tool in his hands.

Cromwell is eloquent in his own language, and, besides, speaks

Latin, French and Italian tolerably well. He lives splendidly; is very liberal both of money and fair words, and remarkably fond of pomp and ostentation in his household and in building.

◆

Thomas Cranmer

Source: Anecdotes and Character of Cranmer by Ralph Morice, his secretary. Camden Soc. *Narratives of the Reformation* (1859) pp. 244–6

Plate 6

Now, as touching his qualities wherewithal he was specially endued, like as some of them were very rare and notable, so ought they not to be put in oblivion. Wherefore among other things it is to be noted that he was a man of such temperature of nature, or rather so mortified, that no manner of prosperity or adversity could alter or change his accustomed conditions: for, being the storms never so terrible or odious, nor the prosperous estate of the time never so pleasant, joyous, or acceptable, to the face of [the] world his countenance, diet, or sleep commonly never altered or changed, so that they which were most nearest and conversant about him never or seldom perceived by no sign or token of countenance how th'affairs of the Prince or the realm went. Notwithstanding privately with his secret and special friends he would shed forth many bitter tears, lamenting the miseries and calamities of the world.

Again, he so behaved himself to the whole world, that in no manner of condition he would seem to have any enemy, although in very deed he had both many great and secret enemies, whom he always bore with such countenance and benevolence that they could never take good opportunity to practice their malice against him but to their great displeasure and hindrance in th'end. And as concerning his own regard towards slanders and reproach by any man to him imputed or impinged, such as entirely knew him can testify that very little he esteemed or regarded the brute[1] thereof, by cause he altogether travailed evermore from giving of just occasion of detraction. Whereupon grew and proceeded that notable quality or virtue he had: to be beneficial unto his enemies, so that in that respect he would not acknown to have any enemy at all. For whosoever he had been that had reported evil of him or otherways wrought or done to him displeasure, were the reconciliation never so mean or simple on the behalf of his adversary, if he had any thing at all relented, the matter was both pardoned and clearly forgotten, and so voluntarily cast into the satchel of oblivion behind the back part, that it was more clear now out of memory, than it was in mind before it was either commenced or committed; insomuch that if any such person should have had any suit unto him afterwards, he might well reckon and be as sure to obtain (if by any means he might lawfully do it) as any other of his special friends. So that on a time I do remember that D. Hethe late Archbishop of York, partly misliking this his overmuch lenity by him used, said unto him, 'My Lord, I now know how to win all things at your hands well enough.' 'How so?' (quoth my Lord). 'Marry,' (said D. Hethe,) 'I perceive that I must first attempt to do unto you some notable displeasure, and then by a little relenting obtain of you what I can desire.' Whereat my Lord bit his lip, as his manner was when he was moved, and said: 'You say well; but yet you may be deceived. Howbeit, having some consideration so to do, I may not alter my mind and accustomed condition, as some would have me to do.'

---

[1] noise, i.e. tenor.

Edward VI

Source: Giralamo Cardano, an Italian physician, visiting the King in September or October, 1552, quoted in Burnet *History of the Reformation* (1829) ii. p. 3

Plate 7

All the graces were in him. He had many tongues when he was yet but a child; together with the English, his natural tongue, he had both Latin and French; nor was he ignorant, as I hear, of the Greek, Italian and Spanish, and perhaps some more. But for the English, French, and Latin, he was exact in them and apt to learn everything. Nor was he ignorant of logic, of the principles of natural philosophy, nor of music. The sweetness of his temper was such as became a mortal, his gravity becoming the majesty of a King, and his disposition suitable to his high degree. In sum, that child was so bred, had such parts, was of such expectation that he looked like a miracle of a man. These things are not spoken rhetorically and beyond the truth, but are indeed short of it. He was a marvellous boy. When I was with him he was in the fifteenth year of his age, in which he spake Latin as politely and as promptly as I did. . . . And indeed the ingenuity and sweetness of his disposition had raised in all good and learned men the greatest expectation of him possible. He began to love the liberal arts before he knew them; and to know them before he could use them: and in him there was such an attempt of nature, that not only England, but the world has reason to lament his being so early snatched away. How truly was it said of such extraordinary persons, that their lives are short and seldom do they come to be old. He gave us an essay of virtue, though he did not live to give a pattern of it. When the gravity of the King was needful, he carried himself like an old man; and yet he was always affable and gentle, as became his age. He played on the lute, he meddled in affairs of state; and for bounty he did in that emulate his father; though he, even when he endeavoured to be too good, might appear to have been bad: but there was no ground of suspecting any such thing in the son, whose mind was cultivated by the study of philosophy.

✦

Mary I

Source: Giacomo Soranzo, the Venetian Ambassador, 18 August 1554. *Cal. S.P. Venetian*, v. p. 532

Plate 10

The Most Serene Madame Mary is entitled Queen of England and of France, and Defendress of the Faith. She was born on 18th Feb. 1515 [1516 N.S.] so she yesterday completed her 38th year and six months. She is of low stature, with a red and white complexion, and very thin; her eyes are white and large, and her hair reddish; her face is round, with a nose rather low and wide; and were not her age on decline, she might be called handsome rather than the contrary. She is not of a strong constitution, and of late she suffers from headache and serious affection of the heart, so that she is often obliged to take medicine, and also to be blooded. She is of very spare diet, and never eats until 1 or 2 p.m., although she rises at daybreak, when, after saying her prayers and hearing mass in private, she transacts business incessantly, until after midnight, when she retires to rest; for she chooses to give audience not only to all the members of her Privy Council, and to hear from them every detail of public business, but also to all other persons who ask it of her. Her Majesty's countenance indicates great benignity and clemency, which are not belied by her conduct, for although she has had many enemies, and though so many of them were by law condemned to death, yet had the executions depended solely on her Majesty's will, not one of them perhaps would have been enforced; but deferring to her Council in everything she in this matter likewise complied with the wishes of others rather than with her own. She is endowed with excellent ability, and more than moderately read in Latin literature, especially with regard to Holy Writ, and besides her native tongue she speaks Latin, French, and Spanish, and understands Italian perfectly, but does not speak it. She is also very generous, but not to the extent of letting it appear that she rests her chief claim to commendation on this quality.

She is so confirmed in the Catholic religion that although the King her brother and his Council prohibited her from having mass celebrated according to the Roman Catholic ritual, she nevertheless had it performed in secret, nor did she ever choose by any act to assent to any other form of religion, her belief in that in which she was born being so strong that had the opportunity offered she would have displayed it at the stake. Her Majesty takes great pleasure in playing on the lute and spinet, and is a very good performer on both instruments; and indeed before her accession she taught many of her maids of honour. But she seems to delight above all in arraying herself elegantly and magnificently. . . . She also makes great use of jewels in which she delights greatly, and although she has a great plenty of them left her by her predecessors, yet were she better supplied with money than she is, she would doubtless buy many more.

❖

Elizabeth I

i. *Source:* Paul Hentzner, *A Journey into England in the Year M.D.XCVIII* (translated by Horace Walpole for the Aungervylle Society 1757) p. 31

Plates 11 and 25

We arrived next at the Royal Palace of Greenwich, reported to have been originally built by Humphrey, Duke of Gloucester, and to have received very magnificent additions from Henry VII. It was here Elizabeth, the present Queen, was born, and here she generally resides; particularly in summer, for the delightfulness of its situation. We were admitted, by an order Mr Rogers had procured from the Lord Chamberlain, into the Presence Chamber, hung with rich tapestry, and the floor, after the English fashion, strewed with hay,[1] through which the Queen commonly passes in her way to Chapel: at the door stood a Gentleman dressed in velvet, with a gold chain, whose office was to introduce to the Queen any person of distinction, that came to wait on her: it was Sunday when there is usually the greatest attendance of nobility. In the same hall were the Archbishop of Canterbury, the Bishop of London, a great number of Counsellors of State, Officers of the Crown, and Gentlemen, who waited the Queen's coming out; which she did from her own apartment when it was time to go to prayers, attended in the following manner:

First went Gentlemen, Barons, Earls, Knights of the Garter, all richly dressed and bare-headed; next came the Chancellor, bearing the Seals in a red-silk purse, between two: one of which carried the Royal Sceptre, the other the Sword of State, in a red scabbard, studded with golden *Fleurs de Lis*, the point upwards: Next came the Queen, in the sixty-fifth year of her age, as we were told, very majestic; her face oblong, fair, but wrinkled; her eyes small, yet black and pleasant; her nose a little hooked; her lips narrow, and her teeth black (a defect the English seem subject to, for their too great use of sugar); she had in her ears two pearls, with very rich drops; she wore false hair, and that red; upon her head she had a small crown, reported to be made of some of the gold of the celebrated Lunebourg Table.[2] Her bosom was uncovered, as all the English Ladies have it, till they marry; and she had on a necklace of exceeding fine jewels; her hands were small, her fingers long, and her stature neither tall nor low; her air was stately, her manner of speaking mild and obliging. That day she was dressed in white silk, bordered with pearls of the size of beans, and over it a mantle of black silk, shot with silver threads; her train was very long, the end of it borne by a marchioness; instead of a chain, she had an oblong collar of gold and jewels. As she went along in all this state and

<hr />

[1] He probably means Rushes [original note].
[2] At this distance of time, it is difficult to say what this was [original note].

magnificence, she spoke very graciously, first to one, then to another, whether foreign ministers, or those who attended for different reasons, in English, French and Italian; for, besides being well skilled in Greek, Latin, and the languages I have mentioned, she is mistress of Spanish, Scotch and Dutch: whoever speaks to her, it is kneeling; now and then she raises some with her hand. While we were there, W. Slawata, a Bohemian Baron, had letters to present to her; and she, after pulling off her glove, gave him her right hand to kiss, sparkling with rings and jewels, a mark of particular favour: wherever she turned her face, as she was going along, everybody fell down on their knees. The Ladies of the Court followed next to her, very handsome and well-shaped, and for the most part dressed in white; she was guarded on each side by the Gentlemen Pensioners, fifty in number, with gilt battleaxes. In the Antichapel next the Hall where we were, petitions were presented to her, and she received them most graciously, which occasioned the acclamation of, *Long Live Queen Elizabeth!* She answered it with, *I thank you, my good people!* In the Chapel was excellent music; as soon as it and the service was over, which scarce exceeded half an hour, the Queen returned in the same state and order, and prepared to go to dinner.

ii. *Source:* Naunton, *Fragmenta Regalia* (1641) pp. 3–13

She was of person tall, of hair and complexion fair, and therewith well favoured, but high nosed, of limbs and features neat, and which added to the lustre of these external graces, of a stately and majestic comportment, participating in this, more of her father, than of her mother, who was of an inferior alloy-plausible, or as the French hath it, more debonair, and affable, virtues, which might well suit with majesty, and which descending as hereditary to the daughter, did render her of a more sweeter temper, and endeared her more to the love and liking of the people, who gave her the name and fame of a most gracious and popular Prince. . . .

The principal note of her reign will be, that she ruled much by faction, and parties which she herself both made, upheld and weakened, as her own great judgement advised for I do disassent from the common and received opinion, that my Lord of Leicester was absolute and alone in her grace; and though I come somewhat short of the knowledge of these times, yet that I may not err nor shoot at random, I know it from assured intelligence that it was not so, for proof whereof amongst many. . . . I will relate both a story and therein a known truth, and 'twas thus: Bowyer the Gent. of the Black Rod, being charged by her express command, to look precisely to all admissions to the Privy-Chamber; one day stayed a very gay Captain (and a follower of my Lord of Leicester) from entrance, for that he was neither well-known, nor a sworn servant to the Queen; at which repulse, the Gent. (bearing high on my Lord's favour), told him that he might perchance procure him a discharge. Leicester coming to the contestation said publicly which was none of his wonted speeches, that he was a knave, and should not long continue in his office, and so turning about to go to the Queen, Bowyer (who was a bold Gent. and well beloved) stepped before him, and fell at her Majesty's feet, relates the story, and humbly craves her grace's pleasure, and whether my Lord of Leicester was King, or her Majesty Queen; whereunto she replied (with her wonted oath) 'God's death my Lord, I have wished you well, but my favour is not so locked up for you that others shall not participate thereof, for I have many servants unto whom I have and will at my pleasure bequeath my favour, and likewise resume the same, and if you think to rule here, I will take course to see you forth coming: I will have here but one Mrs and no Mr and look that no ill happen to him [Bowyer], lest it be severally required at your hands', which so quailed my Lord of Leicester, that his feigned humility was long after one of his best virtues. . . .

From whence, and in many more instances, I conclude that she was absolute and sovereign Mrs of her graces, and that those to whom she distributed her favours were never more than tenants at will and stood on no better terms than her princely pleasure, and their good behaviour.

And this also I present as a known observation, that she was though very capable of counsel, absolute enough in her own resolution, which was ever apparent even to her last, and in that of her still aversion to grant Tyrone the least drop of her mercy, though earnestly and frequently advised thereunto, yea wrought [unitedly]

Michèle Brown.

Elm Tree Books. 1977

ISBN 0-241 89635 5

KETTNER'S BOOK OF THE TABLE
by E S DALLAS.

Centaur press LTD.   1968.

09000000066 2 001

_____

THE GOLDEN AGE OF COOKERY,
TOM BRIDGE.   1983.
Ross Anderson Publications.
ISBN 0-86360-008-5.

by her whole Council of State, with very many reasons; and as the state of her kingdom then stood, I may speak it with assurance, necessitated arguments.

If we look into her inclination as it was disposed to magnificence or frugality, we shall find in them many notable considerations, for all her dispensations were so poised, as though discretion and justice had both decreed to stand at the beam, and see them weighed out in due proportion. . . .

Her rewards chiefly consisted in grants, and leases of offices and places of judicature, but for ready money, and in great sums, she was very sparing; which we may partly conceive, was a virtue rather drawn out of necessity, than her nature; for she had many layings out, and as her wars were lasting, so their charge increased to the last period. . . .

We are naturally prone to applaud the times behind us, and to vilify the present, for the concurrent of her fame carries it to this day how royally and victoriously she lived and died without the grudge and grievance of her people, yet the truth may appear without retraction from the honour of so great a Princess. It is manifest she left more debts unpaid taken upon credit of her Privy Seals than her progenitors did or could have taken up that were an 100 years before her, which was no inferior piece of state to lay the burthen on that house which was best able to bear it at a dead lift, when neither her receipts could yield her relief, at the pinch, nor the urgency of her affairs endure the delays of Parliamentary assistance, and for such aids it is likewise apparent that she received more, and that with the love of her people, then any two of her predecessors, that took most, which was a fortune strained out of her subjects, through the plausibility of her comportment, and (as I would say without offence) the prodigal distribution of her grace to all sorts of subjects, for I believe no Prince living, that was so tender of honour, and so exactly stood for the preservation of sovereignty was so great a courtier of the people, yea of the Commons, and that stooped and declined low in presenting her person to the public view as she passed in her progress and perambulations and in her ejaculations of her prayers on the people. . . .

Moreover it will be a true note of her providence, that she would always listen to her profit: for she would not refuse the information of meanest personages, which proposed improvement ... of which there is a notable example of one Camarthen an Under-Officer of the Custom-house who observing his time, presented her with a paper, showing how she was abused in the under-renting of the Customs, and therewith humbly desired her Majesty to conceal him, for that it did concern two or three of her great Counsellors whom Customer Smith had bribed with £2,000 a man so to lose the Queen £20,000 per annum; which being made known to the Lords, they gave strict order that Carmarthen should not have access to the back stairs, but at last her Majesty smelling the craft, and missing Carmarthen, she sent for him back, and encouraged him to stand to his information, which the poor man did so handsomely, that within the space of ten years he [Customer Smith] was brought to double his rent, or leave the Custom to new Farmers; so that we may take this also in consideration, that there were of the Queen's Council which were not in the catalogue of saints.

❖

William Cecil, Lord Burghley

Source: Naunton, *Fragmenta Regalia* (1641) p. 17

Plate 12

I come now to the next, which was Secretary William Cecil, for on the death of the old Marquis of Winchester, he came up in his room, a person of a most subtle, and active spirit.

He stood not by the way of constellation, but was wholly inten-tive to the service of his Mrs and his dexterity, experience and merit therein, challenged a room in the Queen's favour, which eclipsed the others' overseeming greatness, and made it appear that there were others steered, and stood at the helm besides himself, and more stars in the firmament of grace, than *Ursa Major*.

He was born as they say, in Lincolnshire, but as some aver, upon knowledge of a younger brother, of the Cecils of Hertfordshire, a family of my own knowledge, though now private, yet of no mean antiquity; who being exposed, and sent to the City, as poor gentlemen use to do their sons, became to be a rich man on London Bridge, and purchased in Lincolnshire, where this man was born.

He was sent to Cambridge, and then to the Inns of Court, and so came to serve the Duke of Somerset, in the time of his protectorship as Secretary, and having a pregnancy to high inclinations, he came by degrees to a higher conversation, with the chiefest affairs of State and Counsels, but on the fall of the Duke, he stood some years in umbrage, and without employment,[1] till the State found they needed his abilities, and although we find not that he was taken into place, during Mary's reign, unless (as some say) towards the last, yet the Council several times made use of him, and in the Queen's entrance, he was admitted Secretary of State, afterwards he was made Mr of the Court of Wards, then Lord Treasurer, a person of most excellent abilities, and indeed the Queen began to need and seek out men of both Guards, and so I conclude to rank ... this great instrument amongst the Togatie,[2] for he had not to do with the sword, more than as the great pay-master, and contriver of the war, which shortly followed, wherein he accomplished much, through his theoretical knowledge at home and his intelligence abroad, by unlocking the counsels of the Queen's enemies.

❖

[1] Naunton was incorrect here, since Cecil remained as Secretary of State for the rest of Edward VI's reign, and was employed on some official missions early in Mary's reign.
[2] The peace party.

Sir Francis Walsingham

Source: Naunton, *Fragmenta Regalia* (1641) p. 22

Plate 14 (a)

Sir Francis Walsingham ... was a gentleman at first, of a good house, and of a better education, and from the University travelled for the rest of his learning; doubtless he was the only linguist of his times, how to use his own tongue whereby he came to be employed in the chiefest affairs of State.

He was sent Ambassador to France, and stayed there legarlong[1] in the heat of the Civil-wars, and at the same time that Monsieur was here a suitor to the Queen, and if I be not mistaken he played the very same part there, as since Gundamore [Gondomar] did here: at his return he was taken principal Secretary, and for one of the great engines of State, and of the times, high in his Mrs the Queen's favour, and a watchful servant over the safety of his Mrs. ...

I must again profess that I have read many of his letters, for they are commonly sent to my Lord of Leicester, and of Burleigh, out of France, containing many fine passages, and secrets yet if I might have been beholding to his cyphers, they would have told pretty tales of the times ... with one observation more, that he was one of the greatest always of the Austerian embracements, for both himself, and Stafford that preceded him, might well have been compared to him in the Gospel, that sowed his tares in the night; so did they their seeds in division, in the dark, and as it is a likely report, that they father on him at his return, the Queen speaking to him with some sensibility of the Spanish designs on France: 'Madam,' he answered, 'I beseech you be content, and fear not, the Spaniards have a great appetite and an excellent digestion, but I have fitted him with a bone for these 20 years, that your Majesty should have

[1] Ambassador for a long time.

no cause to doubt him, provided that if the fire chance to slake, which I have kindled, you will be ruled by me, and cast in some of your fuel which will revive the flame.'

❖

Robert Dudley, Earl of Leicester

Source: Naunton, *Fragmenta Regalia* (1641) p. 13

Plate 13

It will be out of doubt, that my Lord of Leicester was one of the first whom she made Master of the Horse, he was the youngest son then living of the Duke of Northumberland, beheaded *primo Mariae*, and his father was that Dudley which our histories couple with Empson ... [who] was executed the first year of Henry VIII. ...

He was a very goodly person, tall, and singularly well featured, and all his youth well favoured, of a sweet aspect, but high fore-headed which (as I should take it) was of no discommendation, but towards his latter, and which with old men was but a middle age, he grew high coloured, so that the Queen had much of her father, for excepting some of her kindred and some few that had handsome wits in crooked bodies, she always took personages in the way of election for the people hath it to this day, 'King Henry loved a man'.

Being thus in her grace, she called to mind the sufferings of his ancestors, both in her father's and sister's reigns, and restored his, and his brother's blood, creating Ambrose the elder, Earl of Warwick, and himself Earl of Leicester, and as he was *ex primiciis* or of her first choice, so he rested not there, but long enjoyed her favour, and therewith what he listed, till time and emulation, the companions of greatness, resolved of his period, and to colour him at his sitting in a Cloud [at Conebury] not by so violent a death, or by the fatal sentence of Judicature, as that of his father and grandfather's was, but as it is supposed by that poison which he had prepared for others, wherein they report him a rare artist.

I am not bound to give credit to all vulgar relations, or to the libels of his time ... but which binds me to think him no good man amongst other things of known truth, is that of my Lord of Essex his death in Ireland, and the marriage of his Lady, which I forbear to press, in regard he is long since dead, and others living whom it may concern.

To take him in the observation of his letters and writings, which should best set him off, for such as have fallen into my hands, I never yet saw a style or phrase more seemingly religious, and fuller of the strains of devotion, and were they not sincere, I doubt much of his well-being, and I fear he was too well seen in the aphorisms, and principles of Nicolas the Florentine, and in the reaches of Caesar Borgia. . . .

He was sent Governor by the Queen to the revolted states of Holland, where we read not of his wonders, for they say, he had more of Mercury, then he had of Mars, and that his device might have been without prejudice to the great Caesar, *Veni, vidi, redivi*.

Sir Walter Ralegh

Source: Naunton, *Fragmenta Regalia* (1641) p. 33

Plate 15 (a)

Sir Walter Ralegh was one that it seems fortune had picked out of purpose, of whom to make an example, and to use as her tennis ball, thereby to show what she could do for she tossed him up of nothing, and to and fro to greatness, and from thence down to little more than to that wherein she found him a bare gentleman, and not that he was less, for he was well descended, and of good alliance; but poor in his beginnings: and for my Lord of Oxford's jests of him to jacks and upstarts, we all know it savoured more of emulation and his honour, than of truth; and it is a certain note of the times, that the Queen in her choice never took in her favour a mere viewed man, or a mechanic. . . .

His approaches to the University and Inns of Court were the grounds of his improvement, but they were rather extrusions than sieges, or settings down, for he stayed not long in a place, and being the youngest brother and the house diminished in his patrimony, he foresaw his destiny, that he was first to rule through want and disability to subsist otherwise before he came to a repose and as the stone doth by long lying gather moss. He was the first that did expose himself in the Land Service of Ireland, a militia which did not then yield him food and raiment, for it was ever very poor, nor dared he to stay long there, though shortly after he came thither again under the command of my Lord Gray, but with his own colours flying in the field, having in the interim cast a mere chance, both in the Low Countries, and in the voyage to sea; and if ever man drew virtue out of necessity, it was he, and therewith was he the great example of industry, and though he might have taken the merchant to himself, *per mare terras currit mercator ad Indos* he might also have said, and truly with the philosopher, *omnia mea mecum porto*, for it was a long time before he could brag of more than he carried at his back, and when he got on the winning side, it was his commendations that he took pains for it, and underwent many various adventures for his after perfection, and before he came into the public note of the world. . . .

He had in the outward man a good presence, in a handsome and well compacted person, a strong natural wit, and a better judgement, with a bold and plausible tongue, whereby he could set out his parts to the best advantage, and these he had by the adjuncts of some general learning, which by diligence he enforced to a great augmentation, and perfection, for he was an indefatigable reader, where by sea or land, and none of the best observers both of men and of the times, and I am somewhat confident, that among the second causes of his growth, that there was variance between him and my Lord General Gray, in his second descent into Ireland, was principal for it, drew them both over to the Council table there to plead their own causes, where what advantage he had in the case, in controversy I know not, but he had much the better in the manner of telling his tale, insomuch as the Queen and the Lords took no slight mark of the man, and his parts for from thence he came to be known, and to have access to the Lords, and then we are not to doubt how such a man would comply to progression, and whether or no my Lord of Leicester had then cast a good word for him to the Queen, which would have done him no harm, I do not determine, but true it is, he had gotten the Queen's ear in a trice, and she began to be taken with his election, and loved to hear his reasons to her demands, and the truth is she took him for a kind of oracle, which nettled them all, yea those that he relied on, began to take this his sudden favour for an alarm, and to be sensible of their own supplantation, and to project him, which made him shortly after sing, 'Fortune my foe, why dost thou frown', so that finding his favour declining, and falling into a recess, he undertook a new peregrination to leave that *terra infirma* of the Court for that of the waves, and by declining himself, and by absence to expel his and the passion of his enemies, which in Court was a strange device of recovery, but that he then knew there was some ill office done him, yet he durst not attempt to remedy it, otherwise than by going aside thereby to teach envy a new way of forgetfulness, and not so much as think of him. Howsoever he always had it in mind, never to forget himself and his device took so well and in his return he came in as rams do, by going backward with the greater strength, and so continued to the last, great in her favour and Captain of her Guard, where I must leave him, but with this observation, though he gained much at the Court he took it not out of the Exchequer, or merely out of the Queen's purse but by his wit and by the help of the prerogative, for the Queen was never profuse in delivering out of her treasure, but paid most and many of her servants part in money, and the rest with grace, which as the case stood, was then taken for good payment leaving the arrears of recompense due for their merit, to her great successor, which paid them all with advantage.

❧

Robert Devereux, Earl of Essex

Source: Naunton, *Fragmenta Regalia* (1641) p. 36

Plate 14 (b)

There was in this young Lord, together with a goodly person a kind of urbanity innovate courtesy, which both won the Queen, and too much took up the people to gaze on the new adopted son of her favour; and as I go along, it will not be amiss to take into observation, two notable quotations: the first was a violent indulgence of the Queen's, which is incident to old age, where it encounters with a pleasing and suitable object towards this great Lord, which argued a non-perpetuity, the second was a fault in the object of her grace, my Lord himself, who drew in too fast like a child sucking on an over uberous nurse, and had there been a more decent decorum observed in both, or either of these, without doubt the unity of their affections had been more permanent, and not so in, and out, as they were, like an instrument well tuned, and lapsing to discord.

The greater error of the two, though unwilling, I am constrained to impose on my Lord of Essex, and rather on his youth, and none of the least of the blame on those that stood sentinel about him, who might have advised better, but that like men intoxicated with hopes, they likewise had sucked in with the most of their Lord's receipts, and so like Caesars would have all or none. . . .

My Lord of Essex, even of those that truly loved and honoured him, was noted for too bold an engrosser, both of fame and favour, and of this . . . I shall present the truth of a passage yet in memory.

My Lord of Mountjoy, who was another child of her favour, being newly come and then but Sir Charles Blount . . . had the good fortune to run one day very well at the Tilt and the Queen was therewith so well pleased, that she sent him in token of her favour a Queen at Chess in gold, richly enamelled which his servants had the next day fastened unto his arm, with a crimson ribbon, which my Lord of Essex, as he passed through the Privy Chamber, espying with his cloak cast under his arm, the better to command it to the view, enquired what it was, and for what cause there fixed: Sir Fulke Greville told him it was the Queen's favour, which the day before, and next after the Tilting, she had sent him; whereat my Lord of Essex in a kind of emulation and as though he would have limited her favour said, 'Now I perceive every fool must have a favour'. This bitter and public affront came to Sir Charles Blount's ear, at which he sent him the challenge which was accepted by my Lord and they met near Marybone[1] Park, where my Lord was hurt in the thigh, and disarmed; the Queen missing of the men was very curious to learn the truth but at last it was whispered out, she swore by God's death it was fit that some one or other should take him down and teach him better manners, otherwise there would be no rule with him. . . .

Now . . . at last, and with much ado, he obtained his own ends [the command in Ireland], and therewith his fatal destruction, leaving the Queen and the Court, where he stood impregnable and firm in her grace, to men that had long fought, and waited their times to give him the trip, and could never find any opportunity but this of his absence, and of his own creation, and those are true observations of his appetite and inclinations, which were not of any true proportion, but hurried and transported with an over-desire and thirstiness for fame, and that deceitful fame of popularity, and to help on his catastrophe, I observed likewise two sorts of people that had a hand in his fall: first was the soldiery which all flock unto him, as it were foretelling a mortality, and are commonly of blunt and too rough counsels . . . the other sort were of his family, his servants and his own creatures such as were bound by safety and obligations of fidelity, to have looked better after the steering of that boat, wherein they themselves were carried and not to have suffered it to fleet and run on ground with those empty sails of tumor of popularity and applause. Methinks one honest man or other, which had but the brushing of his clothes, might have whispered in his ear, My Lord look to it, this multitude that follows you, will either devour you or undo you, do not strive to over-rule all, for it will cost hot water, and it will procure envy, and if your

[1] i.e. Marylebone

genius must have it so, let the Court and the Queen's presence be your station, for your absence must undo you, but as I have said, they have sucked too much of their Lord's milk, and instead of withdrawing, they drew the coals of his ambition and infused into him too much of the spirit of glory . . . there were some of insufferable natures about him, that towards his last gave desperate advice such as his integrity abhorred and his fidelity forbade.

✦

Sir Francis Drake

Source: Letter of Don Francisco da Zarate to Don Martin Enriquez, Viceroy of New Spain, in *New Light on Drake* (ed. Z. Nuttall, Hakluyt Society, 1914) p. 201

Plate 15 (b)

Realejo, Nicaragua, 16th of April, 1579

I sailed out of the port of Acapulco on the 23rd of March and navigated until Saturday, the 4th of April, on which date, half an hour before dawn, we saw, by moonlight, a ship very close to ours. Our steersman shouted that she was to get out of the way and not come alongside of us. To this they made no answer, pretending to be asleep. The steersman then shouted louder, asking them where their ship hailed from. They answered 'From Peru', and that she was 'of Miguel Angel', which is the name of a well-known captain of that route. . . .

The ship of the adversary carried her bark at her prow as though she were being towed. Suddenly, in a moment, she crossed our poop, ordering us 'to strike sail' and shooting seven or eight arquebus shots at us.

We thought this as much of a joke as it afterwards turned out to be serious.

On our part there was no resistance, nor had we more than six of our men awake on the whole boat, so they entered our ship with as little risk to themselves as though they were our friends. They did no personal harm to any one, beyond seizing the swords and keys of the passengers. Having informed themselves as to who were on board ship, they ordered me to go in their boat to where their general was—a fact I was glad of, as it appeared to me that it gave me more time in which to recommend myself to God. But in a very short time we arrived where he was, on a very good galleon, as well mounted with artillery as any I have seen in my life.

I found him promenading on deck and, on approaching him, I kissed his hands. He received me with a show of kindness, and took me to his cabin, where he bade me be seated and said: 'I am a friend of those who tell me the truth, but with those who do not I get out of humour. Therefore you must tell me (for this is the best road to my favour) how much silver and gold does your ship carry?' I said to him, 'None'. He repeated his question. I answered, 'None, only some small plates that I use and some cups—that is all that is in her.' He kept silent for a while, then renewing the conversation asked me if I knew Your Excellency. I said, 'Yes' . . . .

This General of the Englishmen is a nephew of John Hawkins and is the same who, about five years back, took the port of Nombre de Dios. He is called Francisco Drac, and is a man of about 35 years of age, low of stature, with a fair beard, and is one of the greatest mariners that sail the seas, both as a navigator and as a commander. His vessel is a galleon of nearly four hundred tons, and is a perfect sailor. She is manned with a hundred men, all of service, and of an age for warfare, and all are as practised therein as old soldiers from Italy could be. Each one takes particular pains to keep his arquebus clean. He treats them with affection, and they treat him with respect. He carries with him nine or ten cavaliers, cadets of English noblemen. These form a part of his council, which he calls together for even the most trivial matter, although he takes advice from no one. But he enjoys hearing what they say and afterwards issues his orders. He has no favourite.

The aforesaid gentleman sits at his table, as well as a Portuguese pilot, whom he brought from England, who spoke not a word during the whole time I was on board. He is served on silver dishes with gold borders and gilded garlands, in which are his arms. He carries all possible dainties and perfumed waters. He said that many of these had been given to him by the Queen.

None of these gentlemen took a seat or covered his head before him, until he repeatedly urged him to do so. This galleon of his carries about thirty heavy pieces of artillery and a great quantity of firearms with the requisite ammunition and lead. He dines and sups to the music of viols. He carries trained carpenters and artisans, so as to be able to careen the ship at any time. Besides being new, the ship has a double lining. I understood that all the men he carries with him receive wages, because, when our ship was sacked, no man dared take anything without his orders. He shows them great favour, but punishes the least fault. He also carries painters who paint for him pictures of the coast in its exact colours. . . .

I managed to ascertain whether the General was well liked, and all said that they adored him.

❖

POLITICAL

and

CONSTITUTIONAL

The Court of Star Chamber

i. Shakespeare illustrates here the popular conception of Star Chamber in the sixteenth century, that it dealt primarily with riot and the preservation of good order.

Source: W. Shakespeare, *The Merry Wives of Windsor* I. i. 1.

Justice Shallow: Sir Hugh, persuade me not; I will make a Star Chamber matter of it; if he were twenty Sir John Falstaffs, he shall not abuse Robert Shallow, esquire.

Slender: In the county of Gloucester, justice of the peace and *Coram.*

Shallow: Ay, cousin Slender, and *Custalorum.*

ii. *Source:* Lord Bacon, *History of King Henry VII* (ed. Lumby, 1621) p. 15.

According to the lord chancellor's admonition, there was that Parliament divers excellent laws ordained, concerning the points which the King recommended.

First, the authority of the star-chamber, which before subsisted by the ancient common laws of the realm, was confirmed in certain cases by act of Parliament. This Court is one of the sagest and noblest institutions of this kingdom. For in the distribution of courts of ordinary justice, there was nevertheless always reserved a high and pre-eminent power to the King's council, in causes that might in example or consequence concern the state of the commonwealth; and if they were criminal, the council used to sit in the chamber called the star-chamber; if civil, in the white chamber or white-hall. And as the chancery had the Pretorian powers for equity, so the star-chamber had the Censorian powers for offences under the degree of capital. This Court of star-chamber is compounded of good elements, for it consisteth of four kinds of persons —counsellors, peers, prelates and chief judges. It discerneth principally of four kinds of causes—forces, frauds, crimes various of stellionate [fraudulence], and the inchoations or middle acts towards crimes capital or heinous, not actually committed or perpetrated. But that which was principally aimed at by this act was force, and the two chief supports of force, combination of multitudes and maintenance or headship of great persons.

❖

Cardinal Morton's Fork

Source: Holinshed, *Chronicle* (ed. 1808) ii. p. 532

The clergy was of two sorts, the one shewing themselves as they were wealthy, seemly and comely; the other pretending that which was not, poverty, bareness and scarcity, but both were of one mind, and devised all the ways they could to save their purses. The first being called alleged that they were daily at great charges in keeping of hospitalities, in maintaining themselves, their house and families, besides extraordinaries which daily did grow and increase upon them, and by that means they were bare and poor, and prayed they be borne with all and pardoned for that time. The other sort alleged that their livings were but small and slender and scarce able to maintain themselves with all which compelled them to go bare and live a hard and poor life, and therefore [they having nothing] prayed that they might be excused. The Bishop [Morton] when he heard them at full and well considered thereof, very wittily and with a pretty dilemma answered them both, saying to the first: 'It is true you are at great charges, are well beseen in your apparel, well mounted upon your fair palfreys and have your men waiting upon you in good order; your hospitality is good and your daily expenses are large, and you are for the same well reported amongst your neighbours; all which are plain demonstrations of your wealth and ability, otherwise you would not be at such voluntary charges. Now having store to spend in such order, there is no reason but that to your Prince you should much more be well willing and ready to yield yourselves contributory and dutiful, and therefore you must pay.' To the other sort he said: 'Albeit your livings be not of the best, yet good, sufficient, and able to maintain you in better estate than you do employ it, but it appeareth that you are thrifty and frugal men, and what others do voluntarily spend in apparel, house and family, you warily do keep and have it lie by you; and therefore it is good reason that of your store you should spare with a good will and contribute to your Prince, wherefore be contented, for you shall pay.' And so by this pretty dilemma he reduced them to yield a good payment to the King.

◆

The Breach With Rome

i. Catherine of Aragon defends herself before the Papal Legate, 1529

Source: Cavendish: *Life and Death of Thomas Wolsey* (ed. 1827) p. 213

The Court being thus furnished and ordered, the judges commanded the crier to proclaim silence; then was the judges' commission, which they had of the Pope, published and read openly before all the audience there assembled. That done, the crier called the King, by the name of 'King Henry of England, come into the Court,' etc. With that the King answered and said, 'Here, my lords!' Then he called also the Queen, by the name of 'Catherine Queen of England, come into the Court,' etc; who made no answer to the same, but rose up incontinent out of her chair, where as she sat, and because she could not come directly to the King for the distance which severed them, she took pain to go about unto the King, kneeling down at his feet in the sight of all the Court and assembly, to whom she said in effect, in broken English, as followeth:

'Sir,' quoth she, 'I beseech you for all the loves that hath been between us, and for the love of God, let me have justice and right; take of me some pity and compassion, for I am a poor woman and a stranger born out of your dominion; I have here no assured friend, and much less impartial counsel; I flee to you as to the head of justice within this realm. Alas! sir, wherein have I offended you, or what occasion of displeasure have I designed against your will and pleasure, intending, as I perceive, to put me from you? I take God and all the world to witness, that I have been to you a true, humble, and obedient wife. . . .

'This twenty years I have been your true wife or more, and by me ye have had divers children, although it hath pleased God to call them out of this world, which hath been no default in me. And when ye had me at the first, I take God to be my judge, I was true maid, without touch of man; and whether this be true or no, I put it to your conscience. If there be any just cause by the law that ye can allege against me, either of dishonesty or any other impediment, to banish and put me from you, I am well content to depart to my great shame and dishonour; and if there be none, then here I most lowly beseech you let me remain in my former estate, and receive justice at your hands. . . .

'I most humbly require you, in the way of charity, and for the love of God, who is the just judge, to spare me the extremity of this new Court, until I may be advertised what way and order my friends in Spain will advise me to take. And if ye will not extend to me so much indifferent favour, your pleasure then be fulfilled, and to God I commit my cause!'

And with that she rose up, making a low curtsey to the King, and so departed from thence. Many supposed that she would have resorted again to her former place; but she took her way straight out of the house, leaning (as she was wont always to do) upon the arm of her general receiver, called Master Griffith. And the King being advertised of her departure, commanded the crier to call her again, who called her by the name of 'Catherine Queen of England, come into the Court,' etc. With that quoth Master Griffith, 'Madam, ye be called again.' 'On, on,' quoth she; 'it maketh no matter, for it is no impartial Court for me, therefore I will not tarry. Go on your ways.' And thus she departed out of that Court, without any farther answer at that time, or at any other, nor would ever appear at any other Court after.

ii. The Preamble to the Act in Restraint of Appeals, 1533

This preamble contains the essence of Thomas Cromwell's political philosophy.

Source: Statutes of the Realm, iii. p. 427

Where by divers sundry old authentic histories and chronicles it is manifestly declared and expressed that this realm of England is an empire, and so hath been accepted in the world, governed by one Supreme Head and King having the dignity and royal estate of the imperial Crown of the same, unto whom a body politic, compact of all sorts and degrees of people divided in terms and by names of Spiritualty and Temporalty, be bounden and owe to bear next to God a natural and humble obedience; he being also institute and furnished by the goodness and sufferance of Almighty God with plenary, whole, and entire power, pre-eminence, authority, prerogative, and jurisdiction to render and yield justice and final determination to all manner of folk residents or subjects within this his realm, in all causes, matters, debates, and contentions happening to occur, insurge, or begin within the limits thereof, without restraint or provocation to any foreign princes or potentates of the world. . . .

iii. The Act of Supremacy, 1534

Source: Statutes of the Realm, iii. p. 492

Albeit the King's Majesty justly and rightfully is and ought to be the Supreme Head of the Church of England, and so is recognized by the clergy of this realm in their Convocations; yet nevertheless for corroboration and confirmation thereof, and for increase of virtue in Christ's religion within this realm of England, and to repress and extirp all errors, heresies, and other enormities and abuses heretofore used in the same, Be it enacted by authority of this present Parliament that the King our Sovereign Lord, his heirs and successors kings of this realm, shall be taken, accepted, and reputed the only Supreme Head in earth of the Church of England called *Anglicana Ecclesia*[1], and shall have and enjoy annexed and united to the imperial Crown of this realm as well the title and style thereof, as all honours, dignities, pre-eminences, jurisdictions, privileges, authorities, immunities, profits, and commodities, to the said dignity of Supreme Head of the same Church belonging and appertaining: And that our said Sovereign Lord, his heirs and successors kings of this realm, shall have full power and authority from time to time to visit, repress, redress, reform, order, correct, restrain, and amend all such errors, heresies, abuses, offences, contempts, and enormities, whatsoever they be, which by any manner spiritual authority or jurisdiction ought or may lawfully be reformed, repressed, ordered, redressed, corrected, restrained, or amended, most to the pleasure of Almighty God, the increase of virtue in Christ's religion, and for the conservation of the peace, unity, and tranquillity of this realm: any usage, custom, foreign laws, foreign authority, prescription, or any other thing or things to the contrary hereof notwithstanding.

iv. The Execution of Sir Thomas More, 1535

Source: Roper, *Life of Sir Thomas More* (1822) p. 97

And so upon the next morrow, being Tuesday, Saint Thomas his eve, in the year of our Lord 1535, early in the morning came to him Sir Thomas Pope, his singular good friend, on message from the King and his council, that he should before nine of the clock of the same morning suffer death; and that, therefore, he should forthwith prepare himself thereto. 'Master Pope,' quoth Sir Thomas

---

[1] Note the change from the Submission of the Clergy in 1531 when Henry was acknowledged as 'their singular protector, only and supreme lord and, as far as the law of Christ allows, even Supreme Head'.

More, 'for your good tidings I heartily thank you. I have been always much bounden to the King's highness for the benefits and honours that he had still from time to time most bountifully heaped upon me; and yet more bounden am I to his Grace for putting me into this place, where I have had convenient time and space to have remembrance of my end. And so help me God, most of all, Master Pope, am I bounden to his Highness that it pleaseth him so shortly to rid me out of the miseries of this wretched world, and therefore will I not fail earnestly to pray for his Grace, both here, and also in the world to come.' 'The King's pleasure is farther,' quoth Master Pope, 'that at your execution you shall not use many words.' 'Master Pope,' quoth he, 'you do well to give me warning of his Grace's pleasure, for otherwise, at that time, had I purposed somewhat to have spoken; but of no matter wherewith his Grace, or any other, should have had cause to be offended. Nevertheless, whatsoever I intended, I am ready obediently to conform myself to his Grace's commandment, and I beseech you, good Master Pope, to be a mean to his Highness, that my daughter Margaret may be at my burial.' 'The King is content already,' quoth Master Pope, 'that your wife, children and other friends shall have liberty to be present thereat.' 'Oh, how much beholden then,' said Sir Thomas More, 'am I unto his Grace, that unto my poor burial vouchsafed to have so gracious consideration!' Wherewithal Master Pope, taking his leave of him, could not refrain from weeping. Which Sir Thomas More perceiving, comforted him in this wise: 'Quiet yourself, good Master Pope, and be not discomforted, for I trust that we shall once in heaven see each other full merrily, where we shall be sure to live and love together, in joyful bliss eternally.' Upon whose departure, Sir Thomas More, as one that had been invited to some solemn feast, changed himself into his best apparel. Which master lieutenant espying, advised him to put it off, saying, that he that should have it was but a javill[1]. 'What, master lieutenant?' quoth he, 'shall I account him a javill that will do me this day so singular a benefit? Nay, I assure, were it cloth of gold, I should think it well bestowed on him, as Saint Cyprian did, who gave his executioner thirty pieces of gold.' And albeit, at length, through master lieutenant's importunate persuasion, he altered his apparel, yet after the example of

[1] Worthless fellow.

55

the holy Martyr St Cyprian, did he, of that little money that was left him, send an angel of gold to his executioner. And so was he by master lieutenant brought out of the Tower, and from thence led towards the place of execution. Where, going up the scaffold, which was so weak that it was ready to fall, he said merrily to the lieutenant: 'I pray you, master lieutenant, see me safe up, and for my coming down let me shift for myself.' Then desired he all the people thereabout to pray for him, and to bear witness with him, that he should now there suffer death in and for the faith of the holy Catholic church. Which done, he kneeled down, and, after prayers said, turned to the executioner with a cheerful countenance, and said unto him: 'Pluck up thy spirits, man, and be not afraid to do thine office: my neck is very short, take heed, therefore, thou strike not awry, for saving of thine honesty.' So passed Sir Thomas More out of this world to God, upon the very same day which he most desired.

The Pilgrimage of Grace, 1536

i. *The Agrarian Programme of the Rebels, showing how important were economic causes of the revolt.*

Source: Gairdner, *Letters and Papers, Hen. VIII,* xi, 1246

9. That the lands in Westmoreland, Cumberland, Dent, Sedbergh, Furness, and the abbey lands in Mashamshire, Kirkbyshire, Notherdale, may be by tenant right, and the Lords to have, at every change, 2 years' rent for *gressum*, according to the grant now made by the Lords to the Commons there. This is to be done by Act of Parliament.

13. The statute for enclosures and intakes[1] to be put in

[1] Land reclaimed from moor.

execution, and all enclosures and intakes since 4 Hen. VII to be pulled down, except mountains, forests, and parks.

ii. *Source: Chronicle of Edward Hall* (ed. Whibley, 1809) ii. p. 275

All these things [the insurrection in Lincolnshire] thus ended, the country appeased and all things in quiet, the King's Majesty returned and brake up his army.

But see! even within six days following was the King truly certified that there was a new insurrection made by the Northern men, which had assembled themselves into a huge and great army of warlike men, and well appointed both with captains, horse, harness and artillery to the number of 40,000 men, which had encamped themselves in Yorkshire. And these men had each of them to other bound themselves by their oath to be faithful and obedient to his captain; they also declared by their proclamations solemnly made that this their insurrection, should extend no farther but only to the maintenance and defence of the faith of Christ and deliverance of Holy Church, sore decayed and oppressed, and also for the furtherance as well of private as public matters in the realm, touching the wealth of all the King's poor subjects. They named this, their seditious and traitorous voyage, an holy and blessed pilgrimage. They also had certain banners in the field, whereupon was painted Christ hanging on the Cross on the one side and chalice with a painted cake in it on the other side, with divers other banners of like hypocrisy and feigned sanctity. The soldiers also had a certain cognisance or badge embroidered or set upon the sleeves of their coats, which was the similitude of the five wounds of Christ, and in the midst thereof was written the name of our Lord; and this, the rebellious garrison of Satan, with his false and counterfeited signs of holiness set forth and decked themselves, only to delude and deceive the simple and ignorant people.

❧

The Dissolution of the Monasteries

i. The Commissioners' Report to Cromwell on Glastonbury, 1539

Source: *Letters relating to Suppression of Monasteries* (ed. Thomas Wright, Camden Society, 1843) p. 255

Please it your Lordship to be advertised, that we came to Glastonbury on Friday last past, about ten of the clock in the forenoon; and for that the Abbot was then at Sharpham, a place of his a mile and somewhat more from the abbey, we, without any delay, went into the same place, and there examined him upon certain articles. And for that his answer was not then to our purpose, we advised him to call to his remembrance that which he had then forgotten, and so declare the truth, and then came with him the same day to the abbey, and there anew proceeded that night to search his study for letters and books; and found in his study secretly laid, as well a written book or arguments against the divorce of the King's Majesty and the lady dowager, which we take to be a great matter, as also divers pardons, copies of bulls, and the counterfeit life of Thomas Becket in print; but we could not find any letter that was material. And so we proceeded again to his examination concerning the articles we received from your Lordship, in the answers whereof, as we take it, shall appear his cankered and traitorous heart and mind against the King's Majesty and his succession. And so with fair words as we could, we have conveyed him from hence into the tower, being but a very weak man and sickly. And as yet we have neither discharged servant nor monk; but now the Abbot being gone, we will, with as much celerity as we may, proceed to the despatching of them. We have in money £300 and above; but the certainty of plate and other stuff there as yet we know not, for we have not had opportunity for the same, but shortly we intend—God willing—to proceed to the same; whereof we shall ascertain your Lordship as shortly as we may.

This is also to advertise your Lordship, that we have found a fair chalice of gold, and divers other parcels of plate, which the Abbot had hid secretly from all such commissioners as have been there in times past; and as yet he knoweth not that we have found the same. It may please your Lordship to advertise us of the King's pleasure by this bearer, to whom we shall deliver the custody and keeping of the house, with such stuff as we intend to leave there convenient to the King's use. We assure your Lordship it is the goodliest house of that sort that ever we have seen. We would that your Lordship did know it as we do; then we doubt not but your Lordship would judge it a house meet for the King's Majesty and for no man else: which is to our great comfort; and we trust verily that there shall never come any double hood within that house again.

Also this is advertise your Lordship, that there is never a doctor within that house; but there be three bachelors of divinity, which be but meanly learned, as we can perceive. And thus Our Lord preserve your good Lordship.

From Glastonbury, the 22nd day of September, 1539

Yours to command,
Richard Pollard
Thomas Mayle
Richard Layton

To the right honourable
and their singular good
lord, my Lord Privy Seal,
this be delivered

ii. Translation of the Deed of Surrender of Furness Abbey, 1537

Source: Guide-book to Furness Abbey

To all the faithful in Christ, to whom these presents shall come, I, Roger, by the providence of God, Abbot of the monastery of St Mary of Furness, in the county of Lancaster, and the convent of the same send greeting, goodwill, and benediction in the Lord. Know Ye, that we the said Abbot and convent with our unanimous and full assent and consent, particularly for divers special considerations moving us interiorly thereto, and also for the use and defence of this kingdom, and for the good and safe government of this distant portion of the realm aforesaid, have freely given, granted, and surrendered up into the hands of the Lord and King, that now is, Henry VIII, by the grace of God, King of England and France, defender of the Faith, Lord of Ireland, and head upon earth of the Anglican Church, have surrendered our monastery of Furness aforesaid, and also the site and foundation of the same, and all the goods, chattels, jewels, and church ornaments of the same, and also the debts, actions, and other things whatsoever, unto us, or any of us, or unto the said monastery, appertaining, belonging or owing, and also all manner of domains, castles, manors, lands, tenements, advowsons of churches and chantries, knights' fees, rents, reversions, liberties, and services, with all our hereditaments whatsoever, in the counties of York and Lancaster, or elsewhere in the realm of England and Ireland and in the Isle of Man, to have and to hold. . . .

In witness whereof we have, with our unanimous and full assent and consent, affixed our common seal to these presents. Given in the Chapter House of our said monastery, the ninth day of April, in the twenty-eighth year of the reign of our said lord the King, and in the year of our Lord and Saviour, 1537.

By me, Roger, Abbot of Furness. By me, Brian Garner, Prior. By me, John Thornton, &c. &c.

❖

The Statute of Six Articles, 1539

This shows the Catholic reaction and Royal orthodoxy. The statute was repealed in 1547 at the beginning of the reign of Edward VI.

Source: Statutes of the Realm, iii. p. 379

. . . The King's most royal Majesty, of his most excellent goodness not only commanded that the said articles should deliberately and advisedly by his said Archbishops, Bishops, and other learned men of his clergy be debated, argued, and reasoned, and their opinions therein to be vouchsafed in his own princely person to descend and come into his said high Court of Parliament and Council, and there like a Prince of most high prudence and no less learning opened and declared many things of high learning and great knowledge touching the said articles, matters, and questions, for an unity to be had in the same; whereupon, after a great and long deliberate and advised disputation and consultation had and made concerning the said articles, as well by the consent of the King's Highness as by the assent of the Lords spiritual and temporal and other less learned men of his clergy in their Convocation and by the consent of the Commons in this present Parliament assembled, it was and is finally resolved accorded, and agreed in manner and form following, that is to say: First, that in the most blessed Sacrament of the Altar, by the strength and efficacy of Christ's mighty word, it being spoken by the priest, is present really, under the form of bread and wine, the natural body and blood of our Saviour Jesu Christ, conceived of the Virgin Mary, and that after the consecration there remaineth no substance of bread and wine, nor any other substance but the substance of Christ, God and man: Secondly, that communion in both kinds is not necessary *ad salutem* by the law of God to all persons; and that it is to be believed and not doubted of but that in the flesh under form of bread is the very blood, and with the blood under form of wine is the very flesh, as well apart as though they were both together: Thirdly, that priests after the order of priesthood received as afore may not marry by the law of God: Fourthly, that vows of chastity or widowhood by man or woman made to God advisedly ought to be observed by the law of God, and that it exempteth them from other liberties of Christian people which without that they might enjoy: Fifthly, that it is meet and necessary that private masses be continued and admitted in this the King's English Church and congregation as whereby good Christian people ordering themselves accordingly do receive both godly and goodly consolations and benefits, and it is agreeable also to God's law: Sixthly, that auricular confession is expedient and necessary to be retained and continued, used, and frequented, in the Church of God. . . .

Ket's Rebellion, 1549

The Demands of the Rebels

The differences between the causes of this rebellion and the rebellion in the West are seen clearly from these demands.

Source: Harl. MSS. 304 f. 75. Printed by Russell, *Ket's Rebellion in Norfolk*

We certify your grace that whereas the lords of the manors hath been charged with certe free rent, the same lords hath sought means to charge the freeholders to pay the same rent, contrary to right.

We pray your Grace that no lord of no manor shall common upon the commons. . . .

We pray that reed ground and meadow ground may be at such price as they were in the first year of King Henry VII.

We pray that all marshes that are holden of the King's Majesty by free rent or of any other, may be again at the price that they were in the first year of King Henry VII. . . .

We pray that all freeholders and copyholders may take the profits of all commons, and there to common, and the lords not to common nor take profits of the same. . . .

We pray that copyhold land that is unreasonable rented may go as it did in the first year of King Henry VII, and that at the death of a tenant or at a sale the same lands to be charged with an easy fine as a capon or a reasonable [sum] of money for a remembrance. . . .

We pray that all bond men may be made free, for God made all free with his precious blood-shedding. . . .

We pray that your Grace to give licence and authority by your gracious commission under your great seal to such commissioners as your poor commons hath chosen, or as many of them as your Majesty and your council shall appoint and think meet, for to redress and reform all such good laws, statutes, proclamations, and all other your proceedings, which hath been hidden by your justices of your peace, sheriffs, escheators, and other your officers from your poor commons, since the first year of the reign of your noble grandfather King Henry VII.

We pray that those your officers that had offended your Grace and your commons, and so proved by the complaint of your poor commons, do give unto these poor men so assembled iiijd. every day so long as they have remained there.

We pray that no lord, knight, esquire nor gentleman do graze nor feed any bullocks or sheep if he may spend forty pounds a year by his lands, but only for the provision of his house.

By me, Robt. Kett

   ,, ,,   Thomas Aldryche   Thomas Cod

❖

The Western Rebellion, 1549

This shows the conservative reaction to the changes of the first Act of Uniformity, 1549.

Source: Holinshed, *Chronicles* (ed. 1808) iii. p. 918

The articles of the commons of Devonshire and Cornwall, sent to the King. . . .

FIRST, forsomuch as man, except he be born of water, and the Holy Ghost, can not enter into the kingdom of God, and forsomuch as the gates of heaven be not open without this blessed sacrament of baptism; therefore we will that our curates shall minister this sacrament at all times of need, as well on the week days, as on the holy days.

II. Item, we will have our children confirmed of the Bishop, whensoever we shall within the diocese resort unto him.

III. Item, forsomuch as we constantly believe, that after the priest hath spoken the words of consecration being at mass, there celebrating and consecrating the same, there is [in very reality] the body and blood of our Saviour Jesus Christ God and man, and that no substance of bread and wine remaineth after, but the very self same body that was born of the virgin Mary, and was given upon the cross for our redemption: therefore we will have mass celebrated as it hath been in times past, without any man communicating with the priests, forsomuch as many rudely presuming unworthily to receive the same, put no difference between the Lord's body and other kind of meat; some saying that it is bread before and after, some saying that it is profitable to no man except he receive it: with many other abused terms.

IV. Item, we will have in our churches reservation.

V. Item, we will have holy bread and holy water in the remembrance of Christ's precious body and blood.

VI. Item, we will that our priests shall sing or say with an audible voice, God's service in the quire of the parish churches, and not God's service to be set forth like a Christmas play.

VII. Item, forsomuch as priests be men dedicated to God for ministering and celebrating the blessed sacraments, and preaching of God's word, we will that they shall live chaste without marriage, as Saint Paul did, being the elect and chosen vessel of God, saying unto all honest priests: Be you followers of me.

VIII. Item, we will that the six articles which our sovereign lord King Henry the Eighth set forth in his latter days, shall be used and so taken as they were at that time.

IX. Item, we pray God save King Edward, for we be his both body and goods.

❖

The Books of Common Prayer

The doctrinal changes regarding transubstantiation, the extreme swing from 1549 to 1552, and the compromise of the Elizabethan version are clearly shown in the following extracts from the Communion service. The famous Black Rubric of 1552 is added at the end.

1549	1552, 1559
The Supper of the Lord, and the Holy Communion commonly called The Mass	The order for the Administration of the Lord's Supper or Holy Communion

1549 And when he delivereth the Sacrament of the body of Christ he shall say to every one these words:

> 'The body of our Lord Jesus Christ which was given for thee, preserve thy body and soul unto everlasting life '

And the Minister delivering the Sacrament of the blood, and giving every one to drink once and no more, shall say:

> 'The blood of our Lord Jesus Christ which was shed for thee, preserve thy body and soul unto everlasting life.'

1552 And when he delivereth the bread, he shall say:

> 'Take and eat this in remembrance that Christ died for thee, and feed on him in thy heart by faith, with thanksgiving.'

And the minister that delivereth the cup shall say:

> 'Drink this in remembrance that Christ's blood was shed for thee, and be thankful.'

1559 And when he delivereth the bread, he shall say:

> 'The body of our Lord Jesu Christ which was given for thee, preserve thy body and soul into everlasting life, and take, and eat this, in remembrance that Christ died for thee, feed on him in thine heart by faith with thanksgiving.'

And the minister that delivereth the cup shall say:

> 'The blood of our Lord Jesu Christ which was shed for thee, preserve thy body and soul into everlasting life. And drink this in remembrance that Christ's blood was shed for thee, and be thankful.'

1552 *Rubric at the end of the Communion Service*

. . . 'Whereas it is ordained in the book of common prayer, in the administration of the Lord's supper that the Communicants kneeling should receive the Holy Communion. . . . Lest yet the same kneeling might be thought or taken otherwise, we do declare that it is not meant thereby, that any adoration is done, or ought to be done, either unto the sacramental bread or wine there bodily received, or unto any real and essential presence there being of Christ's natural flesh and blood'. . . .

✦

Edward VI's Will

This was written in Edward VI's own hand, probably about mid-May, 1553. Professor S. T. Bindoff has produced a very persuasive theory that a vital alteration from 'the L. Janes heires masles' to 'the L. Jane and her heires masles' (see Plate 32 for illustration of part of the will, and Appendix for complete text), was made by the Duke of Northumberland, since by this alteration he might hope to continue in power (*History Today*, October 1953).

Source: from the original, by courtesy of the Master and Benchers of the Inner Temple

My devise for the Succession.

For lack of issue of my body to the L. Frances' heirs male, if she have any such issue before my death to the L. Jane and her heirs male, To the L. Katherine's heirs male, To the L. Mary's heirs male, To the heirs male of the daughters which she shall have hereafter then to the L. Margaret's heirs male. For lack of such issue, To the heirs male of the L. Jane's daughters To the heirs male of the L. Katherine's daughters and so forth till you come to the L. Margaret's daughters' heirs male.

2. If after my death the heir male be entered into 18 year[s] old, then he to have the whole rule and governance thereof.

3. But if he be under 18, then his mother to be governess till he enter 18 year[s] old. But to do nothing without the advice and

agreement of 6 [members] of a council to be appointed by my last will to the number of 20.

4. If the mother die before the heir enters into 18 the realm to be governed by the council Provided that after he be 14 year[s] all great matters of importance be opened to him.

Wyatt's Rebellion, 1554

Source: John Stowe, *Chronicle* (ed. 1615) p. 619

In the mean season, to wit the third day of February, about three of the clock in the afternoon, Sir Thomas Wyatt and the Kentish-men marched forward from Deptford towards London with five ensigns, being by estimation about two thousand; and so soon as their coming was perceived, there were shot off out of the White Tower, six or eight shots, but missed them—sometimes shooting over and sometimes short. After knowledge thereof was once had in London, forthwith the drawbridge was cut down, and the bridge gates shut. The mayor and sheriffs, harnessed, commanded each man to shut up their shops and windows and to be ready harnessed at their doors, what chance soever might happen. By this time was Wyatt entered into Kent Street and so by St George's Church into Southwark.

On Shrove Tuesday, the sixth of February, Sir Thomas Wyatt removed out of Southwark toward Kingston, where the bridge was broken and kept on the other side by two hundred men; wherefore Wyatt caused two pieces of ordnance to be laid on the end of the bridge, which so frightened them on the other side that they durst not abide; then caused he three or four of his soldiers to leap into the Thames and to swim to the other side; and they loosed the western barges which lay there tied, and so brought them over; and by that means he passed the water and came that night almost to Brainford, or ever they were descried by the Queen's scouts.

Wyatt hearing the Earl of Pembroke was come into the fields, stayed at Knightsbridge until day, his men being very weary with marching that night and the day before, and also partly feebled and faint, having received small sustenance since their coming out of Southwark restless. There was no small ado in London, and likewise the Tower made great preparation of defence. By ten of the clock the Earl of Pembroke had set his troop of horsemen on the hill in the highway above the new bridge over against St James'; his footmen were set in two battles, somewhat lower and nearer Charing Cross, at the lane turning down by the brick wall from Islingtonward, where he had set also certain other horsemen and he had planted his ordnance upon the hillside. . . . The Queen's whole battle of footmen standing still, Wyatt passed along by the wall toward Charing Cross, where the said horsemen that were there, set upon part of them, but were soon forced back. Wyatt with his men marched still forward all along to Temple Bar, and so through Fleet Street, till he came to the *Belle Sauvage*, an inn nigh unto Ludgate, without resistance, his men going not in any good order or array, most with their swords drawn. Some cried: 'Queen Mary hath granted our request, and given us pardon!' Others said: 'The Queen hath pardoned us!'

Thus some of Wyatt's men—some say it was Wyatt himself— came even to Ludgate and knocked, calling to come in, saying, there was Wyatt, whom the Queen had granted to have their requests; but the Lord William Howard stood at the gate and said: 'Avaunt, traitor! thou shalt not come in here.' Wyatt a while stayed and rested him upon a stall over against the *Belle Sauvage* gate, and at the last seeing he could not get into the city, and being deceived by the aid he hoped for, returned back again, till he came to Temple Bar, where a herald came and said to Master Wyatt: 'Sir, you were best by my counsel to yield; you see this day is gone against you.' Wyatt, herewith being somewhat astonished, said: 'Well, if I shall needs yield, I will yield me to a gentleman.' And to him Sir Maurice Berkeley came straight and bade him leap up behind him; and another took Thomas Cobham and William Kennet, and so carried them behind them upon their horses to the Court.

❖

Marian Persecutions

The burning of Bishops Latimer and Ridley in Oxford in 1555. They were followed by Archbishop Cranmer in 1556.

Source: John Foxe's *Book of Martyrs* (ed. A. Clarke, 1888) p. 622

Immediately, they were commanded to make ready, which they obeyed with all meekness. Ridley took his gown and tippet and gave it to his brother-in-law, Master Shipside. . . . Some other of his apparel that was little worth he gave away; the bailiffs took other parts; besides, he gave away some other small things to gentlemen standing by, several of whom pitifully wept; to Sir Henry Lea he gave a new groat, and to some of my Lord Williams' gentlemen; some napkins, some nutmegs and ginger, his dial, and such other things as he had about him, to every one that stood next him. Some even plucked the points off his hose, and happy was he that could get any rag of him.

Latimer gave nothing, but very quietly suffered his keeper to pull off his hose, and his other apparel, which was very simple; and now being stripped to his shroud, he seemed as comely a person to them who were present, as one could desire to see; and tho' in his clothes he appeared a withered and crooked old man, he now stood quite upright. . . .

Then the smith took a chain or iron, and fastened it about both Ridley's and Latimer's middles; and as he was knocking in a staple, Ridley took the chain in his hand, and shook it, and looking aside to the smith said, 'Good fellow, knock it in hard, for the flesh will have his course.' Then his brother brought him gunpowder in a bag, and would have tied it about his neck, but Ridley asked what it was. His brother said, 'Gunpowder'. Then said he, 'I will take it to be sent of God, therefore I will receive it as sent of him. And have you any,' said he, 'for my brother?' meaning Latimer. 'Yea, sir, that I have,' said his brother. 'Then give it to him,' said he, 'lest you come too late.' So his brother went, and carried the gunpowder to Latimer. . . .

Then they brought a faggot, kindled with fire and laid it down at Ridley's feet. To whom Latimer spake in this manner: 'Be of good comfort, brother Ridley, and play the man; we shall this day light such a candle by God's grace in England as I trust shall never be put out.'

And so the fire being kindled, when Ridley saw the fire flaming up towards him, he cried with a loud voice, 'Lord, into thy hands I commend my spirit; Lord, receive my spirit'; and repeated this latter part often in English, 'Lord, Lord, receive my spirit'. Latimer crying as vehemently on the other side, 'O Father of heaven, receive my soul,' he received the flame as if embracing it. After he had stroked his face with his hands, and, as it were, bathed them a little in the fire, he soon died, as it appears, with very little pain. . . .

But Ridley lingered longer by reason of the badness of the fire, which only burned beneath, being kept down by the wood, which when he felt, he desired them for Christ's sake to let the fire come to him, which when his brother-in-law heard, but not well understood, intending to rid him of his pain, but not well advised what he did, heaped faggots upon him, so that he clean covered him, which made the fire more vehement beneath; so that it burned all his lower parts before it once touched the upper, and that made him leap up and down under the faggots, and often desire them to let the fire come to him, saying, 'I cannot burn.' Which was apparent; for after his legs were consumed, he showed his other side towards us, shirt and all untouched with flame! Yet in all this torment he forgot not to call unto God still, having in his mouth, 'Lord, have mercy upon me,' intermingling his cry, 'let the fire come to me, I cannot burn'. In which pain he suffered till one of the standers-by with his bill pulled off the faggots above, and where Ridley saw the fire flame up, he leaned himself to that side. And when the flame touched the gunpowder, he was seen to stir no more, but burned on the other side, falling down at Latimer's feet.

❖

Loss of Calais, 1558

Source: Grafton, *Chronicle* (ed. 1809) ii. p. 557

At this time, although open hostility and war were between England and France, yet, contrary to the ancient custom afore used, the town of Calais and the forts thereabouts were not supplied with any new accrues of soldiers; and this negligence was not unknown to the enemy, who, long before, had plotted the winning of the said town and country. The French King therefore—being sharply nettled with the late loss of St Quentin and a great piece of his country adjoining, and desirous of revenge—thought it not meet to let slip this occasion; and having presently a full army in readiness to employ where most advantage should appear, determined to put in proof, with all speed, the enterprise of Calais; which long, and many times before, was purposed upon.

This design was not so secret but that the deputies of Calais and Guisnes had some intelligence thereof, and informed the Queen and her council accordingly nevertheless either by wilful negligence there, or lack of credit by the Queen's council here, this great case was so slenderly regarded that no provision of defence was made until it was somewhat too late.

The Duke of Guise, being General of the French army, proceeded in this enterprise with marvellous policy. For approaching the English frontier, under cover to victual Boulogne and Ardres, he entered upon the same on a sudden, and took a little bulwark called Sandgate by assault. The next day the Frenchmen, with five double cannons and three culverins, began a battery from the sandhills next Risbank, against the town of Calais; and continued the same by the space of two or three days, until they made a little breach in the wall next unto the Water Gate, which nevertheless was not yet assaultable; for that which was broken in the day, was by them within the town made up again in the night, stronger than before. But the battery was not begun there by the French because they intended to enter in that place; but rather to abuse the English, to have the less regard to the defence of the castle, which was the weakest part of the town, and the place where they were ascertained by their espials, to win an easy entry. . . .

The same night, after the recule[1] of the Frenchmen, whose number so increased in the castle, that the town was not able to resist their force, the Lord Wentworth, deputy of Calais, sent a pursuivant called Guisnes, unto the Duke of Guise, requiring a composition; which, after long debate, was agreed to, upon this sort: that the town with all the great artillery, victuals and munition, should be freely yielded to the French King; that the lives of the inhabitants only should be saved, to whom safe conduct should be granted, to pass where they listed; and that the Lord Deputy, with fifty others, such as the Duke should appoint, should remain prisoners, and be put to their ransom.

The next morning the Frenchmen entered and possessed the town. Thus have ye heard the discourse of the overthrow and loss of the town of Calais, an enterprise which was begun and ended in less than eight days, to the great marvel of the world, that a town of such strength, and so well furnished with all things as that was, should so suddenly be taken and conquered—but most especially in the winter season, when all the country about, being marsh ground, is commonly overflown with water.

The Elizabethan Religious Settlement

I. THE SETTLEMENT OF 1559

i. The Act of Supremacy, 1559

In this Act, Clause V shows the original intention of the government to have a small doctrinal change immediately, and then proceed to an Act of Uniformity in a later session of Parliament after the Act of Supremacy had been enforced. But their hand was forced, as Sir John Neale has shown

[1] gathering together.

(Elizabeth I and her Parliaments 1558–1581, pp. 51 ff.), by the Protestant members of the Commons, and an Act of Uniformity was passed in the same session.

Clause VII abolishes Papal Power, and transfers it to the Crown in Clause VIII, which authorizes the Queen to set up the Court of High Commission. Clause IX empowers the imposition of the Oath of Supremacy.

Source: Statutes of the Realm, iv. 1. p. 350

v. And that it may also please your Highness that it may be enacted by the authority aforesaid, That one Act and Statute made in the first year of the reign of the late King Edward the Sixth, your Majesty's most dear brother, intituled an Act against such persons as shall unreverently speak against the Sacrament of the Body and Blood of Christ, commonly called the Sacrament of the Altar, and for the receiving thereof under both kinds, and all and every branches, clauses and sentences therein contained, shall and may likewise from the last day of this session of Parliament be revived. . . .

vii. And to the intent that all usurped and foreign power and authority, spiritual and temporal, may for ever be clearly extinguished, and never to be used nor obeyed within this realm or any other your Majesty's dominions or countries; may it please your Highness that it may be further enacted by the authority aforesaid, That no foreign prince, person, prelate, state or potentate, spiritual or temporal, shall at any time after the last day of this session of Parliament, use, enjoy or exercise any manner of power, jurisdiction, superiority, authority, pre-eminence or privilege, spiritual or ecclesiastical, within this realm or within any other your Majesty's dominions or countries that now be or hereafter shall be, but from thenceforth the same shall be clearly abolished out of this realm and all other your Highness' dominions for ever; any statute, ordinance, custom, constitutions or any other matter or cause whatsoever to the contrary in any wise notwithstanding.

viii. And that also it may likewise please your Highness that it may be established and enacted by the authority aforesaid, That such jurisdictions, privileges, superiorities and pre-eminences, spiritual and ecclesiastical . . . be united and annexed to the imperial crown of this realm; and that your Highness, your heirs and successors, kings or queens of this realm, shall have full power and authority by virtue of this Act, by Letters Patents under the Great Seal of England, to assign, name and authorize, when and as often as your Highness, your heirs or successors, shall think meet and convenient, and for such and so long time as shall please your Highness, your heirs or successors, such person or persons, being natural-born subjects to your Highness, your heirs or successors, as your Majesty, your heirs or successors, shall think meet, to exercise, use, occupy and execute under your Highness, your heirs and successors, all manner of jurisdiction within these your realms of England and Ireland or any other your Highness' dominions or countries; and to visit, reform, redress, order, correct and amend all such heresies, errors, schisms, abuses, offences, contempts and enormities whatsoever, which by any manner of spiritual or ecclesiastical power, authority or jurisdiction can or may lawfully be reformed, ordered, redressed, corrected, restrained or amended, to the pleasure of Almighty God, the increase of virtue and the conservation of the peace and unity of this realm. . . .

IX. And for the better observation and maintenance of this Act, may it please your Highness that it may be further enacted by the authority aforesaid, That all and every Archbishop, Bishop, and all and every other ecclesiastical person and other ecclesiastical officer and minister, of what estate, dignity, pre-eminence or degree soever he or they be or shall be, and all and every temporal judge, justicer, mayor and other lay or temporal officer and minister, and every other person having your Highness' fee or wages within this realm or any your Highness' dominions, shall make, take and receive a corporal oath upon the Evangelist, before such person or persons as shall please your Highness, your heirs or successors, under the Great Seal of England, to assign and name, to accept and take the same according to the tenor and effect hereafter following, that is to say:

I, A.B., do utterly testify and declare in my conscience, That the Queen's Highness is the only supreme governor of this realm and of all other her Highness' dominions and countries, as well in all spiritual or ecclesiastical things or causes as temporal, and that no foreign prince, person, prelate, state or potentate hath or ought to have any jurisdiction, power, superiority, pre-eminence or authority, ecclesiastical or spiritual, within this realm; and therefore I do utterly renounce and forsake all foreign jurisdictions, powers, superiorities and authorities, and do promise that from henceforth I shall bear faithful and true allegiance to the Queen's Highness, her heirs and lawful successors, and to my power shall assist and defend all jurisdictions, pre-eminences, privileges and authorities granted or belonging to the Queen's Highness, her heirs and successors, or united or annexed to the imperial crown of this realm: so help me God, and by the contents of this Book.

ii. The Act of Uniformity, 1559

Source: Statutes of the Realm, iv. 1. p. 355

Where at the death of our late sovereign lord King Edward the Sixth, there remained one uniform order of common service and prayer and of the administration of sacraments, rites and ceremonies in the Church of England, which was set forth in one book entitled the Book of Common Prayer and administration of sacraments and other rites and ceremonies in the Church of England . . . that the said book, with the Order of Service and of the administration of sacraments, rites and ceremonies, with the alteration and additions therein added and appointed by this Statute, shall stand and be from and after the said Feast of the Nativity of St John the Baptist, in full force and effect, according to the tenor and effect of this Statute; anything in the aforesaid Statute of Repeal to the contrary notwithstanding.

ii. And further be it enacted by the Queen's Highness, with the assent of the Lords and Commons in this present Parliament assembled and by authority of the same, That all and singular ministers in any cathedral or parish church or other place within this realm of England, Wales and the marches of the same or other the Queen's dominions shall from and after the Feast of the Nativity of St John Baptist next coming be bounden to say and use the Matins, Evensong, celebration of the Lord's Supper, administration of each of the sacraments, and all the common and open prayer, in such order and form as is mentioned in the said book so authorized by Parliament in the said fifth and sixth years of the reign of King Edward the Sixth, with one alteration or addition of certain

Lessons to be used on every Sunday in the year, and the form of the Litany altered and corrected, and two sentences only added in the delivery of the sacrament to the communicants, and none other or otherwise. . . .

III. . . . and that from and after the said Feast of the Nativity of St John Baptist next coming all and every person and persons inhabiting within this realm or any other the Queen's Majesty's dominions shall diligently and faithfully, having no lawful or reasonable excuse to be absent, endeavour themselves to resort to their parish church or chapel accustomed, or upon reasonable let thereof to some usual place where common prayer and such service of God shall be used in such time of let, upon every Sunday, and other days ordained and used to be kept as Holy Days, and then and there to abide orderly and soberly, during the time of the common prayer, preachings or other service of God there to be used and ministered; upon pain of punishment by the censures of the Church and also upon pain that every person so offending shall forfeit for every such offence twelve pence, to be levied by the Church-wardens of the parish where such offence shall be done, to the use of the poor of the same parish, of the goods, lands and tenements of such offender, by way of distress.

2. THE TREATMENT OF ROMAN CATHOLICS

i. The Trial and Execution of Father Campion, 1581

It was not until after the Papal Bull of Excommunication of 1570, and more especially the beginning of the Enterprise against England launched by Pope Gregory XIII in 1579, that the laws against the Roman Catholics were tightened considerably. The tragic dilemma of Elizabeth's reign was that the government persecuted the Roman Catholics to ensure the security of the State, while the Roman Catholics saw themselves as martyrs for their religion.

Source: Holinshed, *Chronicles* (ed. 1808) iv. p. 447

On Monday, being the twentieth of November, Edmund Campion, Ralph Sherwin, Lucas Kerbie, Edward Rishton, Thomas

Coteham, Henry Orton, Robert Johnson and James Bosgrave—all these before-named persons were brought unto the high bar at Westminster, where they were severally and altogether indicted upon high treason. . . .

When they had notably convicted them of these matters, which with obstinacy they still denied, they came to the intent of their secret coming over into this realm, which was for the death of her Majesty and overthrow of the whole realm, which should be by domestical rebellion and foreign hostility. . . . 'Yea,' saith Campion, 'never shall you prove this, that we came over either for this intent or purpose, but only for the saving of souls, which mere love and conscience compelled us to do, for that we did pity the miserable estate of our country. But where are your proofs?' said he. 'These are but quirks by the way; our lives, I perceive, standeth upon points of rhetoric, you have shown us the antecedent, now let us have the ergo.' With this continuous course of boldness and impudency Campion and his fellows would grant nothing. . . .

The jury, having wisely and discreetly pondered and searched and seen into the depth of every cause, worthily and deservedly gave them up all guilty of the treasons whereof they were indicted and arraigned. . . .

Edmund Campion was first brought up into the cart; where after the great rumour of so many people somewhat appeased, he spake thus.

First he began—the people then present, expecting his confession—with a phrase or two in Latin, when immediately after he fell into English in this manner: 'I am here brought as a spectacle before the face of God, of angels and of men, satisfying myself to die as becometh a true Christian and catholic man. As to the treasons that have been laid to my charge, I am come here to suffer for, I desire you all to bear witness with me, that thereof I am altogether innocent.' Whereupon answer was made to him by one of the council, that he might not seem to deny the objections against him, having been proved so manifestly in his face, both by sufficient witness and evidence. 'Well, my Lord,' quoth he, 'I am a catholic man and a priest, in that faith have I lived hitherto, and in that faith I do intend to die; and if you esteem my religion treason, then of force I must grant unto you, as for any other treason I will not consent

77

unto.' Then was he moved as concerning his traitorous and heinous offence to the Queen's most excellent Majesty. Whereto he answered: 'She is my lawful Princess and Queen.' There somewhat he drew in his words to himself, whereby was gathered that somewhat he would gladly have spoken, but the great timidity and unstable opinion of his conscience, wherein he was all the time even to the death, would not suffer him to utter it.

ii. The Act of 1585 against Jesuits and seminary priests

The Recusancy fines had already been increased to £20 a month in 1581; this Act shows the government's real fear of the success of the Jesuits.

Source: Statutes of the Realm, iv. 1. p. 706

Whereas divers persons called or professed Jesuits, seminary priests and other priests, which have been and from time to time are made in the parts beyond the seas, according to the order and rites of the Romish Church, have of late years come . . . and daily do come . . . into this realm of England and other the Queen's Majesty's dominions, of purpose (as hath appeared as well by sundry of their own examinations and confessions, as by divers other manifest means and proofs) not only to withdraw her Highness' subjects from their due obedience to her Majesty, but also to stir up and move sedition, rebellion and open hostility within her Highness' dominions, to the great endangering of the safety of her most royal person and to the utter ruin, desolation and overthrow of the whole realm, if the same be not the sooner by some good means foreseen and prevented: for reformation whereof be it enacted . . . That all Jesuits, seminary priests and other priests whatsoever made or ordained . . . by any authority . . . [derived] from the See of Rome, since the feast of the Nativity of St John Baptist in the first year of her Highness' reign, shall within forty days next after the end of this present session of Parliament, depart out of this realm of England and out of all her Highness' realms and dominions.

Source: *John Gerard, the Autobiography of an Elizabethan* (translated by Philip Caraman from the Latin, 1951) p. 107

We went to the torture-room in a kind of solemn procession, the attendants walking ahead with lighted candles.

The chamber was underground and dark, particularly near the entrance. It was a vast place and every device and instrument of human torture was there. They pointed out some of them to me and said I would try them all. Then they asked me again whether I would confess.

'I cannot,' I said.

I fell on my knees for a moment's prayer. Then they took me to a big upright pillar, one of the wooden posts which held the roof of this huge underground chamber. Driven into the top of it were iron staples for supporting heavy weights. Then they put my wrists into iron gauntlets and ordered me to climb two or three wicker steps. My arms were then lifted up and an iron bar was passed through the rings of the second gauntlet. This done, they fastened the bar with a pin to prevent it slipping, and then removing the wicker steps, one by one from under my feet, they left me hanging by my hands and arms fastened above my head. The tips of my toes, however, still touched the ground, and they had to dig away the earth from under them. They had hung me up from the highest staple in the pillar and could not raise me any higher, without driving in another staple.

Hanging like this I began to pray. The gentlemen standing around asked me whether I was willing to confess now.

'I cannot and I will not,' I answered.

But I could hardly utter the words, such a gripping pain came over me. It was worst in my chest and belly, my hands and arms. All the blood in my body seemed to rush up into my arms and hands, and I thought that blood was oozing from the ends of my fingers and the pores of my skin. But it was only a sensation caused by my flesh swelling above the irons holding them. The pain was so intense that I thought I could not possibly endure it, and added to it, I had an interior temptation. Yet I did not feel any inclination or wish to give them the information they wanted. The Lord saw my weakness with the eyes of His mercy, and did not permit me to be tempted beyond my strength. With the temptation He sent me relief. Seeing my agony and the struggle going on in my mind, He gave me this most merciful thought: the utmost and worst they can do is to kill you, and you have often wanted to give your life for your Lord God. The Lord God sees all you are enduring—He can do all things. You are in God's keeping. With these thoughts, God in his infinite goodness and mercy gave me the grace of resignation, and with a desire to die and a hope (I admit) that I would, I offered Him myself to do with me as He wished. From that moment the conflict in my soul ceased, and even the physical pain seemed much more bearable than before, though it must, in fact, I am sure, have been greater with the growing strain and weariness of my body. . . .

Sometime after one o'clock, I think, I fell into a faint. How long I was unconscious I don't know, but I think it was long, for the men held my body up or put the wicker steps under my feet until I came to. Then they heard me pray and immediately let me down again. And they did this every time I fainted—eight or nine times that day—before it struck five. . . .

A little later they took me down. My legs and feet were not damaged, but it was a great effort to stand upright.

3. THE PURITANS

i. The Puritan demands in Convocation, 1563

Source: Strype, *Annals* (1735) i. p. 502

I. That all the Sundays in the year, and principal feasts of Christ be kept holy days, and all other holy days to be abrogated.

II. That in all parish churches the minister in common prayer turn his face toward the people, and there distinctly read the divine service appointed, where all the people assembled may hear and be edified.

III. That in ministering the sacrament of baptism, the ceremony of making the cross in the child's forehead may be omitted, as tending to superstition.

The Chancellors Seat

I   ELIZABETH IN PARLIAMENT

Anno ɦ ꜱ ꜱ ʒ0 octobʒ ɪmaɡo ɦenʒɪcɦ vɪɪ ꜰaᴜᴄɪᴜʒ ꜱeɡe ɪɪᴜꜱᴛɾaꜱꜱɪma
oɾꝺɪnata ꝝ ɦeɾmanɪ ʒɪnᴄk ɫo ʒeɡɪe ꜱ ɪɪɪɪꜱꜱɪaɪɪɪ

2   HENRY VII

Attributed to Michiel Sitium

3 (*a*) HENRY VIII

As a young man
By Joos van Cleve

(*b*) School of Holbein

4 (a) CARDINAL WOLSEY

By Hans Holbein

(b) THOMAS CROMWELL

Copy after Holbein

5   SIR THOMAS MORE AND HIS FAMILY AND DESCENDANTS

Painted by an unknown artist c. 1593, partly based on a drawing by Holbein of 1527

6   ARCHBISHOP CRANMER
By Gerlach Flicke

7 EDWARD VI
School of Holbein

8 THE DUKE OF SOMERSET
Artist unknown

9   THE DUKE OF NORTHUMBERLAND
Artist unknown

10   MARY I

By Hans Eworth

II   ELIZABETH I

Artist unknown. The Queen is depicted standing on the map of
England, a picture painted to commemorate her visit to Sir Henry
Lee at Ditchley, 1593

12 WILLIAM CECIL, LORD BURGHLEY
Artist unknown

13   THE EARL OF LEICESTER
Artist unknown

14 (*a*) SIR
FRANCIS
WALSINGHAM
Artist unknown

(*b*) THE EARL
OF ESSEX
Artist unknown
1597

15 (*a*) SIR
WALTER RALEGH
Artist unknown
1588

(*b*) SIR
FRANCIS DRAKE
Artist unknown

16 HARDWICK HALL

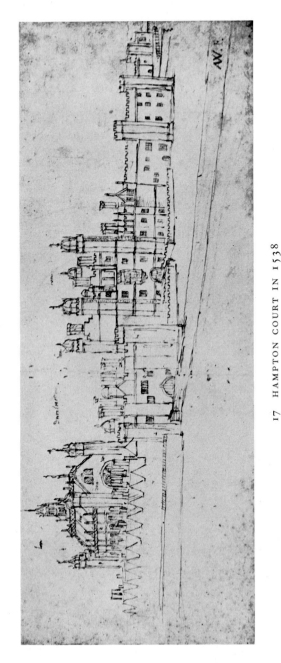

17 HAMPTON COURT IN 1538

18   AN ELIZABETHAN MANOR.   EAST MANOR, BRAMLEY, NEAR GUILDFORD

19   AN ELIZABETHAN STREET. CHIDDINGSTONE, KENT

This illustrates the great rebuilding which took place in England between
1570 and 1640

20   A LONG GALLERY. LANHYDROCK HOUSE, CORNWALL

21 THE HALL. SUTTON PLACE, SURREY

22 (a)   A FOUR POSTER BEDSTEAD OF CARVED AND PAINTED OAK
c. 1600

(b)   A DRAW TABLE. OAK CARVED AND INLAID WITH SYCAMORE
AND BOGWOOD   *c.* 1600

23   A COUNTRY SCENE

By Simon Bening. England must have closely resembled this illustration
from a Flemish source

24   A MARRIAGE FEAST AT BERMONDSEY

By Joris Hofnagel

25   THE COURT IN PROCESSION TO BLACKFRIARS

26 (*a*) LONDON BRIDGE
By Visscher 1616

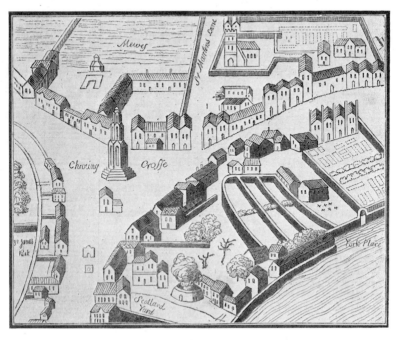

(*b*)　THE VILLAGE OF CHARING IN THE SIXTEENTH CENTURY

27 (*a*) A TUDOR
HOUSEWIFE
By Holbein

(*b*) THE INTERIOR
OF THE
SWAN THEATRE
By Johannes de Witt
1596

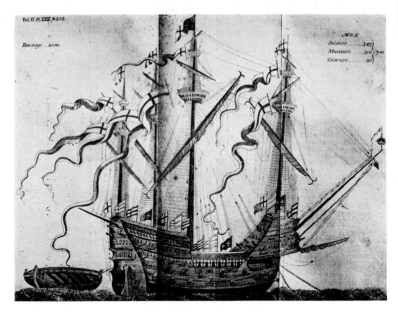

28 (a) 'THE HARRY GRACE-À-DIEU'

(b) 'THE ARK ROYAL'

29 (a) METAL WORKERS

(b) RUFF MAKING

The workers are shown as monkeys 'aping' the follies of the day

30 (a) PRINTING

(b) A WHEELWRIGHT

31 (a) TAILORING

(b) WOOL MAKING

32 EDWARD VI'S DEVISE FOR THE SUCCESSION

Showing the vital alteration at the beginning of the third line.

(See p. 144)

IV. That, forasmuch as divers communicants are not able to kneel during the time of the communion for age, sickness and sundry other infirmities, and some also superstitiously both kneel and knock, that order of kneeling to be left to the discretion of the ordinary within his jurisdiction.

V. That it be sufficient for the minister, in time of saying divine service and ministering the sacraments, to use a surplice, and that no minister say service or minister the sacraments but in a comely garment or habit.

VI. That the use of organs be removed.

ii. The Puritan Admonition to Parliament, 1572

Source: Prothero, *Statutes and Constitutional Documents 1558–1625* (1906) p. 198

Whereas immediately after the last Parliament . . . the ministers of God's holy word and sacraments were called before her Majesty's High Commissioners, and enforced to subscribe unto the articles, if they would keep their places and livings, and some for refusing to subscribe were . . . removed: May it please therefore this honourable and high Court of Parliament . . . to take a view of such causes as then did withhold and now doth the foresaid ministers from subscribing and consenting unto those foresaid articles, by way of purgation to discharge themselves of all disobedience towards the Church of God and their sovereign, and by way of most humble entreaty for the removing away . . . of all such corruptions and abuses as withheld them. . . . Albeit, right honourable and dearly beloved, we have at all times borne with that which we could not amend in this book [of Common Prayer], and have used the same in our ministry, so far forth as we might . . . yet now being compelled by subscription to allow the same and to confess it not to be against the word of God in any point, but tolerable, we must needs say as followeth, that this book is an unperfect book, culled and picked out of that popish dunghill the portuise and mass-book full of all abominations. For some and many of the contents therein be such as are against the word of God. . . .

What should we speak of the Archbishop's Court, sith all men know it, and your wisdoms cannot but see what it is? As all other courts are subject to this by the Pope's prerogative, yea, and by statute of this realm yet unrepealed, so is it the filthy quake-mire and poisoned plash of all the abominations that do infect the whole realm. . . . And as for the commissaries' court, that is but a petty little stinking ditch that floweth out of that former great puddle, robbing Christ's Church of lawful pastors, of watchful seniors and elders, and careful deacons. . . .

And as for the apparel, though we have been long borne in hand, and yet are, that it is for order and decency commanded, yet we know and have proved that there is neither order nor comeliness nor obedience in using it. . . . Neither is the controversy betwixt them and us (as they would bear the world in hand) for a cap, a tippet or a surplice, but for great matters concerning a true ministry and regiment of the Church according to the word. . . . If it might please her Majesty, by the advice of your Right Honourable, in this High Court of Parliament, to hear us by writing or otherwise to defend ourselves, then, such is the equity of our cause that we would trust to find favour in her Majesty's sight. . . . If this cannot be obtained, we will, by God's grace, address ourselves to defend his truth by suffering and willingly lay our heads to the block, and this shall be our peace, to have quiet consciences with our God, whom we will abide for with all patience until he work our full deliverance.

iii. The Queen's Proclamation against Nonconformists, 1573

The presence of the Puritans and their sympathisers in Parliament meant that the Queen had to use Proclamation and the High Commission Court rather than Statute to cope with the Puritan challenge. But it was not until the advent of Whitgift in 1583 as Archbishop of Canterbury that the High Commission was used really effectively (*vide.* iv).

Source: Cardwell, *Documentary Annals* (1839) i. p. 348

The Queen's Majesty being right sorry to understand that the order of Common Prayer . . . is now of late of some men despised and spoken against, both by open preachings and writings, and of some bold and vain curious men new and other rites found out and frequented; whereupon contentions, sects and disquietness doth arise among her people. . . .

For speedy remedy whereof her Majesty straitly chargeth and commandeth all Archbishops and Bishops . . . and all other who have any authority, to put in execution the Act for the Uniformity of Common Prayer and the administration of the sacraments, made in the first year of her gracious reign, with all diligence and severity. . . .

And if any persons shall either in private houses or in public places make assemblies and therein use other rites of Common Prayer and administration of the sacraments than is prescribed in the said Book, or shall maintain in their houses any persons being notoriously charged by books or preachings to attempt the alteration of the said orders, they shall see such persons punished with all severity, according to the laws of this realm, by pains appointed in the said Act.

iv. Lord Burghley protests against Archbishop Whitgift's over-zealous use of High Commission

Source: Strype, Whitgift (1718) iii. pp. 104–7

It may please your Grace, I am sorry to trouble you so often as I do, but I am more troubled myself, not only with many private petitions of sundry ministers, recommended from persons of credit for peaceable persons in their ministry, and yet by complaints to your Grace and other your colleagues in commission greatly troubled; but also I am now daily charged by councillors and public persons to neglect my duty in not staying these your Grace's proceedings so vehement and so general against ministers and preachers, as the Papists are thereby generally encouraged, all ill-disposed subjects animated, and thereby the Queen's Majesty's safety endangered. . . . But now, my good Lord, by chance I am come to the sight of an instrument of twenty-four articles of great length and curiosity, found in a Romish style, to examine all manner of ministers in this time, without distinction of persons. . . . Which I have read, and find so curiously penned, that I think the inquisitors of Spain use not so many questions to comprehend and to trap their preys. I know your canonists can defend these with all their particles, but surely, under your Grace's correction, this judicial and canonical sifting of poor ministers is not to edify or reform. And, in charity, I think they ought not to answer to all these nice points, except they were very notorious offenders in papistry or heresy. Now my good Lord, forbear with my scribbling. I write with a testimony of good conscience. I desire the peace of the Church. I desire concord and unity in the exercise of our religion. I favour no sensual and wilful recusants. But I conclude that, according to my simple judgement, this kind of proceeding is too much savouring of the Romish inquisition, and is rather a device to seek for offenders than to reform any. This is not the charitable instruction that I thought was intended.

◆

The Foreign Situation at Elizabeth's Accession

This assessment should be linked with Gresham's shrewd economic advice to Elizabeth in 1558 (see p. 119 and Appendix).

Source: Gresham to Parry, Antwerp, 16 June 1560, Kervyn de Lettenhove, *Relations politiques des Pays-Bas et de l'Angleterre 1555– 1579*

Her Majesty now needeth not to have any kind of fear of the French King or the King of Spain for any damage they can do to Her Highness any manner of ways. . . . As likewise, whereas Her Majesty oweth one million of ducats, I am right assured that King Philip and the French King oweth each of them apiece 20 millions, so that all things considered, Her Majesty is in better case then the proudest prince of them all. . . . Here is a Scot come from Dieppe, who was there as [at] the 10th of this present, who saith that the French King hath no ships in a readiness and [he] lack[s] both money and men to put in them; and that now he hath more need to have men about himself for to defend the great power that is up in France for to subdue M. de Guise and his brethren.

◆

Elizabeth and Parliament

Some of the main points at issue between Elizabeth and her Parliaments—the Succession, Religion and Trade, and the privilege of freedom of speech which was consequently involved—are illustrated here, together with some of Elizabeth's methods of handling Parliament, ranging from delicate cajoling to wrathful command.

Plate 1

i. Debate on the Queen's Marriage and the Succession, 1566

Source: Commons' Journals, i. pp. 76, 77

November 9, 1566. Mr Vice-Chamberlain declared the Queen's Majesty's express commandment to this House, that they should no further proceed in their suit, but to satisfy themselves with her Highness' promise of marriage. . . .

November 11. Paul Wentworth, one of the burgesses, moved whether the Queen's commandment was not against the liberties: whereupon arose divers arguments, continuing from nine of the clock till two after noon. . . .

November 12. Mr Speaker, being sent for to attend upon the Queen's Majesty at the Court . . . at his coming after ten of the clock, began to show that he had received a special commandment from her Highness to this House, notwithstanding her first commandment, that there should not be further talk of that matter: and if any person thought himself not satisfied but had further reasons, let him come before the Privy Council, there to show them.

November 25. Mr Speaker, coming from the Queen's Majesty,

declared her Highness' pleasure to be that, for her good will to the House, she did revoke her two former commandments, requiring the House no further at this time to proceed in the matter: which revocation was taken of all the House most joyfully with most hearty prayer and thanks for the same.

ii. Speech of the Lord Keeper, 4 April 1571

Source: D'Ewes' Journals q. Prothero, Statutes and Constitutional Documents, 1558–1625 (1906) p. 119

... Her Majesty, having experience of late of some disorder and certain offences (which though they were not punished yet were they offences still and so must be accounted), therefore said, they should do well to meddle with no matters of state but such as should be propounded unto them, and to occupy themselves with other matters concerning the commonwealth.

iii. A Message from the Queen, 22 May 1572

This shows how the House of Commons had not followed the Queen's order (above) and bills had been introduced for religious reform.

Source: Commons' Journals, i. p. 97

May 22, 1572 ... Upon declaration made unto this House by Mr Speaker from the Queen's Majesty, that her Highness' pleasure is that from henceforth no bills concerning religion shall be preferred or received into this House, unless the same should be first considered or liked by the clergy; and further that her Majesty's pleasure is to see the two last bills read in this House touching Rites and Ceremonies; it is ordered, That the same bills shall be delivered unto her Majesty. ...

iv. Speech of Peter Wentworth, 8 February 1576

For this speech Wentworth was committed to the Tower by order of the shocked House of Commons.

Source: D'Ewes' Journals, pp. 236–41 q. Prothero, *Statutes and Constitutional Documents 1558–1625* (1906) p. 120

I was never of Parliament but the last, and the last session, at both which times I saw the liberty of free speech, the which is the only salve to heal all the sores of this commonwealth, so much and so many ways infringed, and so many abuses offered to this honourable council, as hath much grieved me even of very conscience and love to my prince and state. Wherefore to avoid the like, I do think it expedient to open the commodities that grow to the prince and whole state by free speech used in this place. . . . Amongst other, Mr Speaker, two things do great hurt in this place, of the which I do mean to speak: the one is a rumour which runneth about the House, and this it is, 'Take heed what you do, the Queen liketh not such a matter: whosoever preferreth it, she will be offended with him; or the contrary, her Majesty liketh of such a matter: whosoever speaketh against it, she will be much offended with him.' The other: sometimes a message is brought into the House, either of commanding or inhibiting, very injurious to the freedom of speech and consultation. I would to God, Mr Speaker, that these two were buried in hell, I mean rumours and messages. . . .

Now the other was a message, Mr Speaker, brought the last session into the House that we should not deal in any matters of religion, but first to receive from the Bishops. Surely this was a doleful message; for it was as much as to say, 'Sirs, ye shall not deal in God's causes, no, ye shall in no wise seek to advance His Glory'. . . . Certain it is, Mr Speaker, that none is without fault, no, not our noble Queen, since her Majesty hath committed great fault, yea dangerous faults to herself. Love, even perfect love, void of dissimulation, will not suffer me to hide them to her Majesty's peril, but to utter them to her Majesty's safety: and these they are. It is a dangerous thing in a prince unkindly to abuse his or her nobility and people, and it is a dangerous thing in a prince to oppose or bend herself against her nobility and people, yea against most loving and faithful nobility and people. . . .

I so surely think, before God I speak it, that the Bishops were the cause of that doleful message; and I will show you what moveth me so to think. I was, amongst others, the last Parliament sent unto the Bishop of Canterbury, for the Articles of Religion that then passed this House. He asked us, Why we did put out of the book the Articles for the Homilies, Consecrating of Bishops, and such like? 'Surely, sir,' said I, 'because we were so occupied in other matters, that we had no time to examine them how they agreed with the Word of God.' 'What,' said he, 'surely you mistook the matter, you will refer yourselves wholly to us therein?' 'No, by the faith I bear to God,' said I, 'we will pass nothing before we understand what it is, for that were but to make you Popes; make you Popes who list, said I, for we will make you none'.

v. The Queen's answer to a petition by Parliament for the execution of Mary, Queen of Scots, 1586

Source: D'Ewes' Journals pp. 308–402 q. Prothero, Statutes and Constitutional Documents 1558–1625 (1906) pp. 109–111

. . . Since there can be no duer debt than princes' words, which I would observe, therefore I answer to the same. Thus it is; the two petitions which you made unto me do contain two things, my marriage and succession after me. For the first, if I had let slip too much time, or if my strength had been decayed, you might the better have spoke therein; or if any think I never meant to try that life, they be deceived; but if I may hereafter bend my mind thereunto, the rather for fulfilling your request, I shall be therewith very well content. For the second, the greatness thereof maketh me to say and pray, that I may linger here in this vale of misery for your comfort, wherein I have witness of my study and travail for your surety: and I cannot, with *nunc dimittis*, end of my life, without I see some foundation of your surety after my gravestone.

Parliament returned to the attack in a further petition, 'we cannot find there is any possible means to provide for your Majesty's safety, but by the just and speedy execution of the said Queen'.

The Queen's answer, 24 November 1586:

That her Highness, moved with some commiseration for the Scottish Queen, in respect of her former dignity and great fortunes in her younger years, her nearness of kindred to her Majesty and also of her sex, could be well pleased to forbear the taking of her blood, if, by any other means to be devised by her Highness' Great Council of this realm, the safety of her Majesty's person and government might be preserved, without danger of ruin and destruction, and else not; therein leaving them all nevertheless to their own free liberty and dispositions of proceeding otherwise at their choice.

To which the Houses made reply:

That having often conferred and debated on that question, according to her Highness' commandment, they could find no other way than was set down in their petition.

The Queen's second answer:

If I should say unto you that I mean not to grant your petition, by my faith I should say unto you more than perhaps I mean. And if I should say unto you I mean to grant your petition, I should then tell you more than is fit for you to know. And thus I must deliver you an answer answerless.

vi. The Debate on Monopolies, November 1601, and the Queen's answer

Source: *Townsend's Journals.* pp. 230–49

Mr Francis Bacon said: . . . I confess the bill, as it is, is in few words, but yet ponderous and weighty. For the prerogative royal of the prince, for my own part I ever allowed of it, and it is such as I hope shall never be discussed. The Queen, as she is our sovereign, hath both an enlarging and restraining liberty of her prerogative; that is, she hath power by her patents to set at liberty things restrained by statute law or otherwise; and, by her prerogative she may restrain things that are at liberty. . . . But, Mr Speaker (said he, pointing to the bill), this is no stranger in this place, but a stranger in this vestment: the use hath been ever by petition to humble ourselves unto her Majesty and by petition to desire to have our grievances redressed, especially when the remedy toucheth her so nigh in prerogative. All cannot be done at once, neither was it possible since the last Parliament to repeal all. If her Majesty make a patent or a monopoly unto any of her servants, that we must go and cry out against: but if she grant it to a number of burgesses or a corporation, that must stand, and that forsooth is no monopoly. I say, and I say again, that we ought not to deal or meddle with or judge of her Majesty's prerogative. . . .

Dr Bennet: He that will go about to debate her Majesty's prerogative royal, must walk warily. In respect of a grievance out of that city for which I serve, I think myself bound to speak that now which I had not intended to speak before; I mean a monopoly of salt. It is an old proverb, *Sal sapit omnia*; fire and water are not more necessary. But for other monopolies of cards (at which word Sir Walter Ralegh blushed) dice, starch, &c., they are, because monopolies, I must confess, very hateful, though not so hurtful. I know there is a great difference in them; and I think, if the abuse in this monopoly of salt were particularized, this would walk in the fore-rank. . . .

Mr Francis Moore: Mr Speaker, I know the Queen's prerogative is a thing curious to be dealt withal, yet all grievances are not comparable. I cannot utter with my tongue or conceive with my heart the great grievances that the town and country, for which I serve, suffer by some of these monopolies. It bringeth the general profit into a private hand, and the end of all is beggary and bondage to the subjects. We have a law for the true and faithful carrying of leather: there is a patent that sets all at liberty, notwithstanding that statute. And to what purpose is it to do anything by act of Parliament, when the Queen will undo the same by her prerogative? Out of the spirit of humility, Mr Speaker, I do speak it: there is no act of hers that hath been or is more derogatory to her own Majesty, or more odious to the subject, or more dangerous to the commonwealth than the granting of these monopolies. . . .

The following passages occurred in Committee, 21 November:

Sir Robert Wroth: . . . There have been divers patents granted since the last Parliament; these are now in being, viz: the patents for currants, iron, powder, cards, horns, ox-shin bones, train-oil, transportation of leather, lists of cloth, ashes, bottles, glasses, bags, shreds of gloves, aniseed, vinegar, sea-coals, steel, aquavite, brushes, pots, salt, salt-petre, lead, accedence, oil, calamint stone, oil of blubber, fumathoes, or dried pilchers in smoke, and divers others.

Upon reading of the patents aforesaid, *Mr Hackwell of Lincoln's Inn* stood up and asked thus: 'Is not bread there?' 'Bread,' quoth another; 'This voice seems strange,' quoth a third. 'No,' quoth *Mr Hackwell*, 'but if order be not taken for these, bread will be there before the next Parliament.'

On 23 November, the debate was renewed:

Mr Secretary Cecil: If there had not been some mistaking or confusion in the committee, I would not now have spoken. The question was, of the most convenient way to reform these grievances of monopolies: but after disputation, of that labour we have not received the expected fruit. . . . This dispute draws two great things in question; first, the prince's power; secondly, the freedom of Englishmen. I am born an Englishman, and a fellow-member of this House; I would desire to live no day, in which I should detract from either. I am servant of the Queen; and before I would speak or give my consent to a case that should debase her prerogative or abridge it, I would wish my tongue cut out of my head. . . .

For my own part, I like not these courses should be taken. And you, Mr Speaker, should perform the charge her Majesty gave unto you at the beginning of this Parliament not to receive bills of this nature; for her Majesty's ears be open to all grievances, and her hand stretched out to every man's petition. For the matter of access I like it well, so it first be moved and the way prepared. I had rather all the patents were burnt than her Majesty should lose the hearts of so many subjects as is pretended she will.

On 25 November, the Speaker brought the following message to the House:

It pleased her Majesty to command me to attend upon her yesterday in the afternoon, from whom I am to deliver unto you all her Majesty's most gracious message, sent by my unworthy self. . . . It pleased her Majesty to say unto me, that if she had an hundred tongues she could not express our hearty good-wills. And further she said, that as she had ever held our good most dear, so the last day of our or her life should witness it; and that if the least of her subjects were grieved, and herself not touched, she appealed to the throne of Almighty God, how careful she hath been, and will be, to defend her people from all oppressions. She said, that partly by intimation of her council, and partly by divers petitions that have been delivered unto her both going to chapel and also walking abroad, she understood that divers patents, that she had granted, were grievous to her subjects; and that the substitutes of the patentees had used great oppression. But, she said, she never assented to grant anything which was *malum in se*. And if in the abuse of her grant there be anything evil, which she took knowledge there was, she herself would take present order of reformation thereof. I cannot express unto you the apparent indignation of her Majesty towards these abuses. She said her kingly prerogative was tender; and therefore desireth us not to speak or doubt of her careful reformation; for, she said, her commandment given a little before the late troubles (meaning the Earl of Essex's matters) by the unfortunate event of them was not so hindered, but that since that time, even in the midst of her most great and weighty occasions, she thought upon them. And that this should not suffice, but that further order should be taken presently, and not *in futuro* (for that also was another word which I take it her Majesty used), and that some should be presently repealed, some suspended, and none put in execution but such as should first have a trial according to the law for the good of the people. Against the abuses her wrath was so incensed, that she said, that she neither could nor would suffer such to escape with impunity. So to my unspeakable comfort she hath made me the messenger of this her gracious thankfulness and care.

vii. *Elizabeth's golden speech, November, 1601*

She made this very shortly after the Monopolies Debate. This was liable, as most of the Commons must have realized, to be the last time she addressed them.

Source: Somers Tracts (1809) i. p. 244

Mr Speaker, We perceive your coming is to present thanks to us. Know I accept them with no less joy than your loves can have desire to offer such a present, and do more esteem it than any treasure or riches; for those we know how to prize, but loyalty, love, and thanks, I account them invaluable. And though God hath raised me high, yet this I account the glory of my crown, that I have reigned with your loves. This makes me that I do not so much rejoice that God hath made me to be a Queen, as to be a Queen over so thankful a people, and to be the means under God to conserve you in safety and to preserve you from danger. . . . Of myself I must say this: I never was any greedy, scraping grasper, nor a strict, fast-holding prince, nor yet a waster; my heart was never set upon any worldly goods, but only for my subjects' good. What you do bestow on me, I will not hoard up, but receive it to bestow on you again; yea, my own properties I account yours, to be expended for your good, and your eyes shall see the bestowing of it for your welfare. . . .

Mr Speaker, you give me thanks, but I am more to thank you, and I charge you, thank them of the Lower House from me; for, had I not received knowledge from you, I might have fallen into the lapse of an error, only for want of true information. . . . That my grants shall be made grievances to my people, and oppressions be privileged under colour of our patents, our princely dignity shall not suffer. When I heard it, I could give no rest unto my thoughts until I had reformed it. . . . It is not my desire to live or reign longer than my life and reign shall be for your good. And though you have had, and may have, many mightier and wiser princes sitting in this seat, yet you never had, nor shall have any that will love you better.

Mr Speaker, I commend me to your loyal loves, and yours to my best care and your further councils; and I pray you, Mr Controller and Mr Secretary, and you of my council, that before these gentlemen depart into their countries, you bring them all to kiss my hand.

❖

The Rebellion of the Northern Earls, 1569

Source: Holinshed, *Chronicles* (1808) iv. p. 235

On Thursday the ninth of November, Thomas Percy Earl of Northumberland received the Queen's Majesty's letters to repair to the Court. And the same night other conspirators perceiving him to be wavering and unconstant of promise made to them, caused a servant of his, called Beckwith, after he was laid in his bed, to bustle in and to knock at his chamber door, willing him in haste to arise and shift for himself, for that his enemies . . . were about the park and had beset him with great numbers of men. Whereupon he arose and conveyed himself away to his keeper's house. In the same instant they caused the bells of the town to be rung backward, and so raised as many as they could to their purpose. The next night the Earl departed thence to Branspith, where he met with Charles Earl of Westmoreland and other confederates. Then by sundry proclamations, they abusing many of the Queen's subjects, commanded them, in her Highness' name, to repair to them in warlike manner, for the defence and surety of her Majesty's person . . .

Upon Monday the thirteenth of November, they went to Durham with their banners displayed. And to get the more credit among the favourers of the old Romish religion, they had a cross with a banner of the five wounds borne before them, sometime by old Norton, sometime by others. As soon as they entered, they went to the minster, where they tore the bible, communion books and other such as were there. The same night they went again to Branspith. The fourteenth day of the said month they went to Darlington, and there had mass; which the Earls and the rest heard with such lewd devotion as they had. Then they sent their horsemen to gather together such number of men as they could. The fifteenth day the Earls parted; he of Northumberland to Richmond, then to

Northallerton, and so to Boroughbridge; and he of Westmoreland to Ripon, and after to Boroughbridge, where they both met again. ... On the eighteenth day they went to Wetherby and there tarried three or four days, and upon Clifford moor, nigh unto Brainham moor, they mistrusted themselves; at which time they [were] about 2,000 horsemen and 5,000 footmen, which was the greatest number that ever they were. From which they intended to have marched forward toward York, but their minds being suddenly altered, they returned.

The three and twentieth of November, they besieged Barnards Castle, which castle was valiantly defended by Sir George Bowes and Robert Bowes, his brother, the space of eleven days, and then delivered with composition to depart with armour, munition, bag and baggage. In which time the Queen's Majesty caused the said Earls of Northumberland and Westmoreland to be proclaimed traitors, with all their adherents and favourers, the four and twentieth of November. The Lord Scroop, warden of the west marches, calling unto him the Earl of Cumberland and other gentlemen of the country, kept the city of Carlisle. The Earl of Sussex, the Queen's lieutenant-general in the north, published there the like proclamations in effect, as had been published by her Majesty against the said rebels, and also sent out to all such gentlemen as he knew to be her Majesty's loving subjects under his rule; who came unto him with such numbers of their friends, as he was able in five days to make above 5,000 horsemen and footmen. ... And the twentieth of December they came to Hexham, from whence the rebels were gone the night before to Naworth; where they counselled with Edward Dacres concerning their own weakness, and also how they were not only pursued by the Earl of Sussex and others with him, having a power with them of 7,000 men, being almost at their heels; but also by the Earl of Warwick and the Lord Clinton, high admiral of England, with a far greater army of 12,000 men, raised by the Queen's Majesty's commissioners out of the south and middle parts of the realm. ...

The coming forward of these forces caused the rebels so much to quail in courage, that they durst not abide to try the matter with dint of sword. For whereas the Earl of Warwick and the lord admiral, being advanced forward to Darlington, meant the next day to have

sent Robert Glover, then Portcullis and now Somerset herald . . .
unto the rebels, upon such message as for the time and state of
things was thought convenient: the same night advertisements came
from the Earl of Sussex unto the Earl of Warwick and to the lord
admiral that the two Earls of Northumberland and Westmoreland
were fled; as the truth was they were indeed—first from Durham
whither the same Glover should have been sent unto them; and now
upon the Earl of Sussex's coming unto Hexham, they shrank quite
away and fled into Scotland, without bidding their company
farewell. The Earl of Warwick and his power marched on to
Durham. But the Earl of Sussex pursuing those other rebels that
had not means to flee out of the realm, apprehended no small number
of them at his pleasure, without finding any resistance among them
at all.

The fourth and fifth of January did suffer at Durham to the
number of three score and six, constables and others, amongst
whom the alderman of the town and a priest called parson Plomtree
were the most notable. Then Sir George Bowes being made marshall,
finding many to be fautors in the foresaid rebellion, did see them
executed in divers places of the country.

❖

Mary, Queen of Scots

i. Mary writes to Babington, 17 July 1586

Source: Labanoff, *Lettres, etc., de Marie Stuart* (1852) vi. pp. 385–96

Trusty and well beloved, according to the zeal and entire
affection which I have known in you in the common cause of the
religion and of my own in particular, I have ever based my hope
upon you as a chief and most worthy instrument to be employed
in both causes. . . . I cannot but praise, for divers great and im-

portant reasons, too long to recite here, your desire to hinder in time the plans of our enemies who seek to destroy our religion in this realm, and ruin all of us together. For long ago I pointed out to the other foreign Catholic princes, and experience has proved me right, that the longer we delayed intervening from both sides, the greater advantage we give to our opponents to prevail against the said princes, as they have done against the King of Spain; and meanwhile the Catholics here, exposed to all kinds of persecution and cruelty, steadily grow less in numbers, power, and means. . . . Everything being prepared, and the forces, as well within as without, being ready, then you must set the six gentlemen to work and give order that, their design accomplished, I may be in some way got away from here and that all your forces shall be simultaneously in the field to receive me while we await foreign assistance, which must then be brought up with all speed. Now as no certain day can be appointed for the performance of the said gentlemen's enterprise, I desire them to be always near them, or at least at Court, four brave men well horsed to advertise speedily the success of their design, as soon as it is done, to those appointed to get me away from hence, so as to be able to get here before my keeper is informed of the said execution. . . . This plan seems to me the most suitable for this enterprise, so as to carry it out with care for our own safety. To move on this side before we are sure of good foreign help would simply be to risk to no purpose falling into the same miserable fortune as others who have formerly undertaken in this way. . . . (Confirmed as a true copy by Anthony Babington, Nau [Claude de la Nau, Mary's secretary], and Gilbert Curle)

ii. The Execution of Mary

Source: Report to Lord Burghley. Ellis, *Original Letters, Second Series*, iii. p. 116

Her prayer being ended, the executioners, kneeling, desired her Grace to forgive them her death: who answered, 'I forgive you with all my heart, for now, I hope, you shall make an end of all my troubles'. Then they, with her two women, helping her up, began to disrobe her of her apparel: then she, laying her crucifix upon the stool, one of the executioners took from her neck the *Agnus Dei*, which she, laying hands off it, gave to one of her women, and told the executioner he should be answered money for it. Then she suffered them, with her two women, to disrobe her of her chain of pomander beads and all other her apparel most willingly, and with joy rather than sorrow, helped to make unready herself, putting on a pair of sleeves with her own hands which they had pulled off, and that with some haste, as if she had longed to be gone.

All this time they were pulling off her apparel, she never changed her countenance, but with smiling cheer she uttered these words, 'that she never had such grooms to make her unready, and that she never put off her clothes before such a company' . . .

This done, one of the women having a *Corpus Christi* cloth lapped up three-corner-ways, kissing it, put it over the Q. of Sc. face, and pinned it fast to the caule[1] of her head. Then the two women departed from her, and she kneeling down upon the cushion most resolutely, and without any token or fear of death, she spake aloud this Psalm in Latin, *In Te Domine confido, non confundar in eternam*, *etc*. Then, groping for the block, she laid down her head, putting her chin over the block with both her hands, which, holding there still, had been cut off had they not been espied. Then lying upon the block most quietly, and stretching out her arms cried, *In manus tuas, Domine*, *etc*. three or four times. Then she, lying very still upon the block, one of the executioners holding her slightly with one of his hands, she endured two strokes of the other executioner with an axe, she making very small noise or none at all, and not stirring any part of her from the place where she lay: and so the executioner cut off her head, saving one little gristle, which being cut asunder, he lift up her head to the view of all the assembly and bade 'God save the Queen'. Then, her dress of lawn falling off from her head, it appeared as grey as one of threescore and ten years old, polled very short, her face in a moment being so much altered from the form she had when she was alive, as few could remember her by her dead face. Her lips stirred up and down a quarter of an hour after her head was cut off. . . .

Then one of the executioners, pulling off her garters, espied

[1] The back part of a woman's cap.

her little dog which was crept under her clothes, which could not be gotten forth but by force, yet afterward would not depart from the dead corpse, but came and lay between her head and her shoulders, which being imbrued with her blood was carried away and washed.

The Death of Sir Philip Sydney, 1586

Source: Sir Fulke Greville, *Life of Sir Philip Sydney* (ed. 1907) p. 128

Thus they go on, every man in the head of his own troop, and the weather being misty, they fell unawares upon the enemy, who had made a strong stand to receive them, near to the very walls of Zutphen; by reason of which accident their troops fell not only unexpectedly to be engaged within the level of the great shot that played from the ramparts, but more fatally within shot of their muskets, which were laid in ambush within their own trenches. . . . Howsoever by this stand, an unfortunate hand out of those fore-spoken trenches brake the bone of Sir Philip's thigh with a musket shot. The horse he rode upon was rather furiously choleric, than bravely proud, and so forced him to forsake the field, but not his back, as the noblest and fittest bier to carry a martial commander to his grave. In this sad progress, passing along by the rest of the army, where his uncle the General was, and being thirsty with excess of bleeding, he called for drink, which was presently brought him; but as he was putting the bottle to his mouth, he saw a poor soldier carried along, who had eaten his last at the same feast, ghastly casting up his eyes at the bottle; which Sir Philip perceiving, took it from his head before he drank, and delivered it to the poor man with these words: 'Thy necessity is yet greater than mine!'

And when he had pledged this poor soldier, he was presently carried to Arnhem. . . .

The last scene of this tragedy, was the parting between the two brothers; the weaker showing infinite strength in suppressing sorrow and the stronger infinite weakness in expressing of it. So far did invaluable worthiness in the dying brother enforce the living to descend beneath his own worth, and by soundance of childish tears, bewail the public, in his particular loss. . . . And to stop his natural torrent of affection in both, [Sir Philip] took his leave with these admonishing words: 'Love my memory; cherish my friends; their faith to me may assure you they are honest. But above all govern your will and affections by the will and word of your Creator; in me beholding the end of this world, with all her vanities.' And with this farewell desired the company to lead him away. Here this noble gentleman ended the too short scene of his life; in which path whosoever is not confident that he walked the next way to eternal rest, will be found to judge uncharitably. . . . For my own part, I confess, in all I have here set down of his worth and goodness, I find myself still short of that honour he deserved, and I desired to do him.

❖

The Spanish Armada, 1588

Plate 28 (b)

i. Elizabeth's Speech to her troops at Tilbury

Source: Cabala (1691) p. 343

My loving people, we have been persuaded by some that are careful of our safety, to take heed how we commit ourselves to armed multitudes, for fear of treachery. But I assure you, I do not desire to live to distrust my faithful and loving people. Let tyrants fear. I have always so behaved myself that, under God, I have placed my chiefest strength and safeguard in the loyal hearts and good will of my subjects; and therefore I am come amongst you, as you see, at this time, not for my recreation and disport, but being resolved, in the midst and heat of the battle, to live or die amongst you all, to lay down for my God, and for my kingdom, and for my people, my honour and my blood even in the dust. I know I have the body of a weak and feeble woman, but I have the heart and stomach of a King, and of a King of England too, and think foul scorn that Parma or Spain, or any prince of Europe should dare to invade the borders of my realm; to which, rather than any dishonour shall grow by me, I myself will take up arms, I myself will be your general, judge, and rewarder of every one of your virtues in the field. I know, already for your forwardness you have deserved rewards and crowns; and we do assure you, in the word of a prince, they shall be duly paid you.

ii. *Despatches sent to Walsingham from the English Commanders*

Source: State Papers relating to the Defeat of the Spanish Armada (ed. J. K. Laughton) CCXII. 80, CCXIII, 65, 71

Sir,

I will not trouble you with any long letter; we are at this present otherwise occupied than with writing. Upon Friday, at Plymouth, I received intelligence that there were a great number of ships descried off of the Lizard; whereupon, although the wind was very scant, we first warped out of harbour that night, and upon Saturday turned out very hardly, the wind being at south-west; and about three of the clock in the afternoon, descried the Spanish fleet, and did what we could to work for the wind, which by this morning we had recovered, descrying their fleet to consist of 120 sail, whereof there are four galleasses and many ships of great burden.

At nine of the clock we gave them fight, which continued until one. In this fight we made some of them to bear room to stop their leaks; notwithstanding we durst not adventure to put in among them, their fleet being so strong. But there shall be nothing either neglected or unhazarded, that may work their overthrow.

Sir, the captains in her Majesty's ships have behaved themselves most bravely and like men hitherto, and I doubt not will continue, to their great commendation. And so, recommending our good success to your godly prayers, I bid you heartily farewell. From aboard the *Ark*, thwart of Plymouth the 21st of July, 1588.

Your very loving friend,
C. Howard

Sir, the southerly wind that brought us back from the coast of Spain brought them out. God blessed us with turning his back. Sir, for the love of God and our country, let us have with some speed some great shot sent us of all bigness; for this service will continue long; and some powder with it.

RIGHT HONOURABLE,

This bearer came aboard the ship I was in in a wonderful good time, and brought with him as good knowledge as we could wish. His carefulness therein is worthy recompense, for that God has given us so good a day in forcing the enemy so far to leeward as I hope in God the Prince of Parma and the Duke of Sidonia shall not shake hands this few days; and whensoever they shall meet, I believe neither of them will greatly rejoice of this day's service. The town of Calais hath seen some part thereof, whose mayor her Majesty is beholden unto. Business commands me to end. God bless her Majesty, our gracious sovereign, and give us all grace to live in His fear. I assure your Honour this day's service hath much appalled the enemy, and no doubt but encouraged our army. From aboard her Majesty's good ship the *Revenge*, this 29th of July, 1588.

Your honour's most ready to be commanded.

FRA. DRAKE

There must be great care taken to send us munition and victual whithersoever the enemy goeth.

Yours, FRA. DRAKE

iii. An Independent Account

The great German banking family, the Fuggers, regularly received reports from their agents, from which this selection is taken. The new calendar of Pope Gregory XIII had been adopted in 1582 in Catholic Europe, and this accounts for the confusion in dating—ten days had been dropped.

Source: The Fugger News-Letters, second series (ed. Victor von Klarwill) translated L. S. R. Byrne, 1926. pp. 163, 168, 174

Hamburg, June 23, 1588 (O.S.). I simply must tell you that the skipper, Hans Limburger, has arrived here with his vessel from Cadiz. He broke through the embargo, and has a cargo of salt, wine, raisins, cinnamon, and a little sugar. He put out from there on the 20th ult., O.S., and passed Lisbon on the 24th. In the distance he saw the Spanish Armada and sailed abreast of it all day. The next day it was blowing rather hard and he could not see it. He is of opinion that the Armada put out on the 23rd of May Old Style or the 2nd of June New Style and was shaping a course for the Channel. The skipper met an English warship on his way and this brought him into Plymouth, to Drake's Armada. He was entertained by Drake for three days and the English were rejoicing that the Spanish Armada was at sea. Afterwards Captain Drake gave the skipper a permit, so that he might be allowed to pass, and quickly formed an order and put to sea in spite of a contrary wind. If an action is fought, there will be terrible loss of life. On two consecutive days here the sun and moon have been quite bloody. What this signifies the merciful God alone knows. May he defend the Right!

Hamburg, August 3 and 4, 1588. Hans Buttber has arrived off the town in a big ship. He comes through the Channel from San Lucar. He was with Captain Drake for four or five days and joined the Englishman on the 21st, O.S., of last month, just after the latter had had an engagement with the Spanish Armada. From the 21st to the 26th they had skirmished and fired heavily at each other, but they could not board, and the English with their little ships sailed so well and manoeuvred so skilfully, firing meanwhile, that the galleasses could not get at them. Drake captured Don Pedro de

Valdez, Admiral of fourteen vessels, and had him and ten other nobles brought on to his own ship. He gave them a banquet and treated them very handsomely and entertained them besides with trumpets and music. On this ship he took sixty guns and made four hundred and fifty men prisoners. . . .

This noon there comes from Holland a vessel which was at Enkhuizen actually on the last day of July. It brings news that eighteen ships of the Spanish Armada were sunk by gunfire, and eight taken and brought to England. The rest of the Spanish Armada has fled to the French coast. If this is true it will somewhat abate Spanish insolence and give the English fresh courage, though they have no lack of insolence either.

Venice, August 19, 1588. . . . Although his Majesty of Spain was already suffering greatly from gout, his pains redoubled when he heard news how greatly the Spanish Armada had suffered in the storm and how it was somewhat hindered in its operations.

✦

The Attack on Cadiz, 1596

Source: E. Edwards, *The Life of Sir Walter Ralegh* (1868) ii. p. 146

It is not known to whom Ralegh wrote this letter, of which only a part is printed here.

This being agreed on, and both the Generals persuaded to lead the body of the fleet, the charge for the performance thereof [was] (upon my humble suit) granted and assigned unto me.

The Lord Thomas Howard—because the *Meere-Honour*, which he commanded, was one of the greatest ships—was also left behind with the Generals; but being impatient thereof, pressed the Generals to have the service committed unto him, and left the *Meere-Honour* to Mr Dudley, putting himself into the *Nonpareill*. For mine own part, as I was willing to give honour to my Lord Thomas, having both precedency in the army, and being a nobleman whom I much honoured, so yet I was resolved to give and not take example for his service, holding mine own reputation dearest, and remembering my great duty to her Majesty. With the first peep of day, therefore, I weighed anchor, and bare with the Spanish fleet, taking the start of all ours a good distance. . . .

Having, as aforesaid, taken the leading, I was first saluted by the fort called *Philip*, afterwards by the ordnance on the curtain, and lastly by all the galleys, in good order. To show scorn to all which, I only answered first the fort, and afterwards the galleys, to each piece a blurr with a trumpet: disdaining to shoot one piece at any one or all of those esteemed dreadful monsters. The ships that followed beat upon the galleys so thick that they soon betook them to their oars, and got up to join with the galleons in the strait, as aforesaid; and then, as they were driven to come near me, and enforced to range their sides towards me, I bestowed a benediction amongst them.

But the *St Philip*, the great and famous Admiral of Spain, was the mark I shot at; esteeming those galleys but as wasps in respect of the powerfulness of the other; and being resolved to be revenged for the *Revenge*, or to second her with mine own life, I came to anchor by the galleons; of which the *Philip* and *Andrew* were two that boarded the *Revenge*. I was formerly commanded not to board, but was promised fly-boats, in which, after I had battered a while, I resolved to join unto them.

My Lord Thomas came to anchor by me, on the one hand, with the *Lyon*; the *Mary Rose*, on the other, with the *Dreadnaught*; the Marshal[1] towards the side of Puntall; and towards ten of the clock, my Lord General Essex, being impatient to abide far off, hearing so great thunder of ordnance, thrust up through the fleet, and headed all those on the left hand, coming to anchor next unto me on that side; and afterward came in the *Swiftsure*, as near as she could. Always I must, without glory, say for myself, that I held single in the head of all.

Now, after we had beat, as two butts, one upon another almost three hours (assuring your Honour that the volleys of cannon and culverin came as thick as if it had been a skirmish of musketeers), and finding myself in danger to be sunk in the place, I went to my

[1] Sir Francis Vere.

Lord General in my skiff, to desire him that he would enforce the promised fly-boats to come up, that I might board; for as I rid, I could not endure so great battery any long time. My Lord General was then coming up himself; to whom I declared that if the fly-boats came not, I would board with the Queen's ship, for it was the same loss to burn, or sink, for I must endure the one. The Earl finding that it was not in his power to command fear, told me that, whatsoever I did, he would second me in person, upon his honour. My Lord Admiral, having also a disposition to come up at first, but the river was so choked as he could not pass with the *Ark*, came up in person into the *Nonpareill*, with my Lord Thomas.

While I was thus speaking with the Earl, the Marshal who thought it some touch to his great esteemed valour to ride behind me so many hours, got up ahead my ship; which my Lord Thomas perceiving headed him again;—myself being but a quarter of an hour absent. At my return, finding myself from being the first to be but the third, I presently let slip anchor, and thrust in between my Lord Thomas and the Marshal, and went up further ahead than all them before, and thrust my self athwart the channel; so as I was sure none should outstart me again, for that day. My Lord General Essex, thinking his ship's side stronger than the rest thrust the *Dreadnaught* aside, and came next the *Warspight* on the left hand; ahead all that rank, but my Lord Thomas. The Marshal, while we had no leisure to look behind us, secretly fastened a rope on my ship's side towards him, to draw himself up equally with me; but some of my company advertising me thereof, I caused it to be cut off, and so he fell back into his place, whom I guarded, all but his very prow, from the sight of the enemy.

Now if it please you to remember, that having no hope of my fly-boats to board, and that the Earl and my Lord Thomas both promised to second me, I laid out a warp by the side of the *Philip* to shake hands with her (for with the wind we could not get aboard): which when she and the rest perceived, finding also that the *Repulse* (seeing mine) began to do the like, and the Rear-Admiral my Lord Thomas, they all let slip, and ran aground, tumbling into the sea heaps of soldiers, so thick as if coals had been poured out of a sack in many ports at once; some drowned and some sticking in the mud. The *Philip* and the *St Thomas* burnt themselves: the *St*

Matthew and the *St Andrew* were recovered with our boats ere they could get out to fire them. The spectacle was very lamentable on their side; for many drowned themselves; many, half burnt, leapt into the water; very many hanging by the ropes' ends by the ships' side, under the water even to the lips; many swimming with grievous wounds, strucken under water, and put out of their pain: and withal so huge a fire, and such tearing of the ordnance in the great *Philip*, and the rest, when the fire came to them, as, if any man had a desire to see Hell itself, it was there most lively figured. Ourselves spared the lives of all, after the victory; but the Flemings, who did little or nothing in the fight, used merciless slaughter, till they were by myself, and afterward by my Lord Admiral, beaten off. . . .

This being happily finished, we prepared to land the army, and to attempt the town; in which there were, of all sorts, some five thousand foot burghers, one hundred and fifty soldiers in pay, and some eight hundred horse of the gentry and cavalleros of Xerez, gathered together upon the discovery of our fleet two days before, while we were becalmed off Cape St Mary. The horsemen sallied out to resist the landing; but were so well withstood that they most took their way toward the bridge which leadeth into the Main, called Puento Souse; the rest retired to the town, and so hardly followed, as they were driven to leave their horses at the port (which the inhabitants durst not open, to let them in), and so they leapt down an old wall into the suburbs; and being so closely followed by the vanguard of our footmen, as, when the General perceived an entrance there, he thought it was possible for ours to do the like; upon which occasion the town was carried with a sudden fury, and with little loss. . . .

The town of Cales was very rich in merchandize, in plate, and money; many rich prisoners given to the land commanders; so as that sort are very rich. Some had prisoners for sixteen thousand ducats; some for twenty thousand; some for ten thousand; and, besides, great houses of merchandize. What the Generals have gotten, I know least; they protest it is little. For my own part, I have gotten a lame leg, and a deformed.

◆

ECONOMIC and SOCIAL

The Price Revolution

Though contemporaries bemoaned the effects of the Price Rise in the first half of the sixteenth century, the success and wealth it had brought by the end of the century were also obvious.

i. *Source:* Master Hugh Latimer, *Seven Sermons before Edward VI* (ed. E. Arber, *English Reprints*, 1869) p. 38

You landlords, you rent-raisers, I may say you steplords, you unnatural lords, you have for your possessions yearly too much. For that heretofore went for xx or xl pound by year (which is an honest portion to be had *gratis* in one lordship, of another man's sweat and labour) now is it let for fifty or a hundred pound by year.

My father was a yeoman, and had no lands of his own, only he had a farm of three or four pound by year at the uttermost, and thereupon he tilled so much as kept half a dozen men. He had walk for a hundred sheep, and my mother milked thirty kine. He was able and did find the King a harness, with himself and his horse, while he came to the place that he should receive the King's wages. I can remember that I buckled his harness, when he went unto Blackheath field. He kept me to school, or else I had not been able to have preached before the King's Majesty now. He married my sisters with five pound or twenty nobles apiece, so that he brought them up in godliness and fear of God.

He kept hospitality for his poor neighbours. And some alms he gave to the poor, and all this he did of the said farm, where he that now hath it payeth sixteen pound by year or more, and is not able to do anything for his prince, for himself nor for his children, or give a cup of drink to the poor. Thus all the enhancing and rearing goeth to your private commodity and wealth; so that where ye had a single too much, you have that; and since the same, ye have enhanced the rent, and so have increased another too much; so now ye have double too much, which is two too much. But let the preacher preach till his tongue be worn to the stumps, nothing is amended. We have good statutes made for the common wealth as touching commoners, enclosers; many meetings and sessions, but in the end of the matter there cometh nothing forth. Well, well, this is one thing I will say unto you, from whence it cometh I know, even from the devil.

ii. *Source:* T. Wilson, *The State of England* (1600) Camden Miscellany xvi p. 18

It cannot be denied but the Common people are very rich, albeit they be much decayed from the states they were wont to have, for the gentlemen, which were wont to addict themselves to the wars, are now for the most part grown to become good husbands and know [as] well how to improve their lands to the uttermost as the farmer or countryman, so that they take their farms into their hands as the leases expire, and either till themselves or else let them out to those who will give most; whereby the yeomanry of England is decayed and become servants to gentlemen . . . but my young masters the sons of such [yeoman], not contented with their states of their fathers to be counted yeomen and called John or Robert (such an one), but must skip into his velvet breeches and silken doublet and, getting to be admitted into some Inn of Court or Chancery, must ever think scorn to be called any other than gentleman. . . .

Notwithstanding this that the great yeomanry is decayed, yet by this means the communality is increased, 20 now perhaps with their labour and diligence living well and wealthily of that land which our great yeoman held before, who did no other good but maintain beef and brews for such idle persons as would come and eat it, a fine daughter or 2 to be married after with £1000 to some covetous mongrel.

iii. *Source:* W. Harrison, *Description of England,* 1577 (ed. F. J. Furnivall, 1877) p. 238

The furniture of our houses also exceedeth, and is grown in manner even to passing delicacy: and herein I do not speak of the nobility and gentry only, but likewise of the lowest sort in most places of our south country that have anything at all to take to. Certes in noblemen's houses it is not rare to see abundance of arras, rich hangings of tapestry, silver vessels, and so much other plate as may furnish sundry cupboards to the sum oftentimes of a thousand or two thousand pounds at the least, whereby the value of this and the rest of their stuff doth grow to be almost inestimable. Likewise in the houses of knights, gentlemen, merchantmen and some other wealthy citizens, it is not geason[1] to behold generally their great provision of tapestry, Turkey work, pewter, brass, fine linen, and thereto costly cupboards of plate, worth five or six hundred or a thousand pounds to be deemed by estimation. But, as herein all these sorts do far exceed their elders and predecessors, and in neatness and curiosity the merchant all other, so in time past the costly furniture stayed there, whereas now it is descended yet lower even unto the inferior artificers and many farmers, who, by virtue of their old and not of their new leases, have for the most part learned also to garnish their cupboards with plate, their joined beds with tapestry and silk hangings, and their tables with carpets and fine napery, whereby the wealth of our country (God be praised therefore, and give us grace to employ it well) doth infinitely appear. Neither do I speak this in reproach of any man, God is my judge, but to shew that I do rejoice rather to see how God hath blessed us with his good gifts; and whilst I behold how that, in a time wherein all things are grown to most excessive prices and what commodity so ever is to be had is daily plucked from the communality by such as look into every trade, we do yet find the means to obtain and achieve such furniture as heretofore hath been unpossible.

There are old men yet dwelling in the village where I remain which have noted three things to be marvellously altered in England within their sound remembrance.

[1] rare.

One is the multitude of chimneys lately erected, whereas in their young days there were not above two or three, if so many, in most uplandish towns of the realm (the religious houses and manor places of their lords always excepted, and peradventure some great personages), but each one made his fire against a reredos in the hall, where he dined and dressed his meat.

The second is the great (although not general) amendment of lodging; for, said they, our fathers, yea, and we ourselves also, have lain full oft upon straw pallets, on rough mats covered only with a sheet, under coverlets made of dagswain[1] or hopharlots[2] (I use their own terms), and a good round log under our heads instead of a bolster or pillow. If it were so that our fathers or the goodman of the house had within seven years after his marriage purchased a mattress or flock bed, and thereto a sack of chaff to rest his head upon, he thought himself to be as well lodged as the lord of the town, that peradventure lay seldom in a bed of down or whole feathers, so well were they contented, and with such base kind of furniture: which also is not very much amended as yet in some parts of Bedfordshire, and elsewhere, further off from our southern parts. Pillows (said they) were thought meet only for women in childbed. As for servants, if they had any sheet above them, it was well, for seldom had they any under their bodies to keep them from the pricking straws that ran oft through the canvas of the pallet and rased their hardened hides.

The third thing they tell of is the exchange of vessels, as of treen[3] platters into pewter, and wooden spoons into silver or tin. For so common were all sorts of treen stuff in old time that a man should hardly find four pieces of pewter (of which one was peradventure a salt) in a good farmer's house, and yet for all this frugality (if it may be so justly called) they were scarce able to live and pay their rents at their days without selling of a cow or a horse or more, although they paid but four pounds at the uttermost by the year. Such also was their poverty that, if some one odd farmer or husbandman had been at the ale-house, a thing greatly used in those days, amongst six or seven of his neighbours, and there in

[1] Coarse, shaggy cloth.
[2] Coarse coverlet made of shreds.
[3] Wooden.

a bravery, to shew what store he had, did cast down his purse, and therein a noble or six shillings in silver, unto them (for few such men then cared for gold, because it was not so ready payment, and they were oft enforced to give a penny for the exchange of an angel[1]), it was very likely that all the rest could not lay down so much against it; whereas in my time, although peradventure four pounds of old rent be improved to forty, fifty or a hundred pounds, yet will the farmer, as another palm or date tree, think his gains very small toward the end of his term if he have not six or seven years' rent lying by him, therewith to purchase a new lease, besides a fair garnish of pewter on his cupboard, with so much more in odd vessels going about the house, three or four feather beds, so many coverlets and carpets of tapestry, a silver salt, a bowl for wine (if not a whole nest), and a dozen of spoons to furnish up the suite.

2. DEBASEMENT OF THE COINAGE

This was recognized in the sixteenth century as a major cause of the rise in prices.

i. *Source: A Discourse of the Common Weal of this Realm of England*, 1581 (ed. E. Lamond, 1893) p. 104. Probably written by John Hales, famous in Edward VI's reign for his opposition to enclosure.

Knight: Then ye think plainly that this alteration of the coin is the chiefest and principal cause of this universal dearth?
Doctor: Yes, no doubt, and of many of the said griefs that we have talked of, by means of it being the original of all. And that, beside the reason of the thing (being plainly enough of itself), also experience and proof doth make more plain; for even with the alteration of the coin began this dearth; and as the coin appeared, so rose the price of things withal. And this to be true, the few pieces of old coin yet remaining testifieth; for ye shall have, for any of the said coin, as much of any ware either inward or outward as much as ever was wont to be had for the same; and so as the measure is made less, there goeth [the more] some to make up the tale. And because this riseth not together at all mens' hands, therefore some hath great loss, and some other great gains thereby, and that makes

[1] Gold coin worth about 10s.

such a general grudge for the thing. And thus, to conclude, I think this alteration of the coin to be the first original cause that strangers first sold their wares dearer to us; and that makes all farmers and tenants, that reareth any commodity, again to sell the same dearer; the dearth thereof makes the gentlemen to raise their rents, and to take farms into their hands for the better provision, and consequently to enclose more grounds.

ii. *Source:* Master Hugh Latimer, *Seven Sermons before Edward VI* (ed. E. Arber, *English Reprints*, 1869) p. 34. The first sermon of 8 March 1549

We have now a pretty little shilling, indeed a very pretty one. I have but one, I think, in my purse, and the last day I had put it away almost for an old groat, and so I trust some will take them. The fineness of the silver I cannot see. But therein is printed a fine sentence: that is, *Timor Domini fons vitae vel sapientiae.* The fear of the Lord is the fountain of life or wisdom. I would God this sentence were always printed in the heart of the King in choosing his wife, and in all his officers.

3. ENCLOSURE

The substitution of pasture for tillage was the main cause of complaints which went on throughout the sixteenth century—as the following extracts show. Many remedies were suggested, but there was little chance of any of them succeeding while wool-growing remained so profitable.

i. *Source:* Sir Thomas More, *Utopia*, 1516 (translated by G. C. Richards, 1923) p. 13

'Your sheep', said I, 'which are usually so tame and so cheaply fed, are now, it is said, so greedy and wild, that they devour men, and lay waste and depopulate fields, houses and towns. For in those parts of the realm where the finest and therefore most costly wool is produced, these nobles and gentlemen, and even holy Abbots, not satisfied with the revenues and annual profits derived from their estates, and not content with leading an idle life and doing no good to the country, but rather doing it harm, leave no ground to be tilled, but enclose every bit of land for pasture, pull down houses, and destroy towns, leaving only the church to pen the sheep in. And, as if enough English land were not wasted on parks and preserves of game, these holy men turn all human habitations and cultivated land into a wilderness. Thus in order that one insatiable glutton and plague of his native land may join field to field and surround many thousand acres with one ring fence, many tenants are ejected and, either through fraud or violence, are deprived of their goods, or else wearied by oppression are driven to sell. Thus by hook or by crook the poor wretches are compelled to leave their homes—men, women, husbands, wives, orphans, widows, parents with little children and a family not rich but numerous, for farm work requires many hands: away they must go, I say, from their familiar and accustomed homes, and find no shelter to go to. All their household furniture, which would not fetch a great price if it could wait for a purchaser, as it must be thrust out, they sell for a trifle: and soon, when they have spent that in moving from place to place, what remains for them but to steal, and be hung, justly forsooth, or wander about and beg? And yet even then they are put in prison as vagrants, for going about idle, when, though they eagerly offer their labour, there is no one to hire them. For there is no farm work, to which they have been bred, to be had, when there is no plough land left. For one shepherd or herdsman is sufficient for eating up with stock land for whose cultivation many hands were once required, that it might raise crops. And so it is that the price of food has risen in many parts. Nay, the price of wool has grown so high that the poor, who used to make cloth in England, cannot buy it, and so are driven from work to idleness.'

ii. *Source: A Discourse of the Common Weal of this Realm of England*, 1581 (ed. E. Lamond, 1893) p. 15

Husbandman: Marry for these enclosures do undo us all, for they make us pay dearer for our land that we occupy, and causes that we can have no land in manor for our money to put to tillage; all is taken up for pastures, either for sheep or for grazing of cattle. So that I have known of late a dozen ploughs within less compass than 6 miles and about me laid down within these [8] years and where 40 persons had their livings, now one man and his shepherd hath all. Which thing is not the least cause of these uproars, for by these enclosures men do lack livings and be idle; and therefore for very necessity they are desirous of a change, being in hope to come thereby to somewhat; and well assured, howsoever it befall with them, it cannot be no harder with them than it was before. Moreover all things are so dear that by their daily labour they are not able to live.

iii. *Source:* from 'Chrestoleros', in *The Poems, Eng. and Latin, of the Rev. Thomas Bastard, M.A.* (ed. A. B. Grosart, 1880) p. 37. This was written in 1598.

Book III. Epigr. 22. Ad reginam Eliȝabetham

I know where is a thief and long hath been,
Which spoileth every place where he resorts:
He steals away both subjects from the Queen,
And men from his own country of all sorts.
Houses by three, and seven, and ten he razeth,
To make the common glebe, his private land:
Our country Cities cruel he defaceth,
The grass grows green where little Troy did stand,
The forlorn father hanging down his head,
His outcast company drawn up and down,
The pining labourer doth beg his bread,
The ploughswain seeks his dinner from the town.
    O Prince, the wrong is thine, for understand,
    Many such robberies will undo thy land.

4. STATE ACTION

Many of these proposals though pious in intention were never put into effect, while others, like enclosure commissions, show by their frequency their ineffectiveness. But they all serve to reveal the attitude of the Government in the sixteenth century.

i. Limitation of Sheep Farming, 1534

Source: Record Office Calendar vii, 73, quoted in Merriman, *Thomas Cromwell*, i. p. 373

From Thomas Cromwell to Henry VIII

Please it your most royal Majesty to be advertised how that according to your most high pleasure and commandment I have made search for such patents and grants as your Highness and also the most famous King your father—whose soul our Lord pardon—have granted unto Sir Richard Weston, knight, your under treasurer of your exchequer, and the same have sent to your Highness herein closed. It may also please your most royal Majesty to know how that yesterday there passed your Commons a bill that no person within this your realm shall hereafter keep and nourish above the number of 2,000 sheep, and also that the eighth part of every man's land, being a farmer, shall for ever hereafter be put in tillage yearly; which bill, if by the great wisdom, virtue, goodness and zeal that your Highness beareth towards this your realm, might have good success and take good effect among your lords above, I do conjecture and suppose in my poor simple and unworthy judgment, that your Highness shall do the most noble, profitable and most beneficial thing that ever was done to the commonwealth of this your realm, and shall thereby increase such wealth in the same amongst the great number and multitude for your most loving and obedient subjects as never was seen in this realm since Brutus' time. Most humbly prostrate at the feet of your magnificence, I beseech your Highness to pardon my boldness in this writing to your grace; which only proceedeth for the truth, duty, allegiance and love I do bear to your Majesty and the commonwealth of this your realm, as our Lord knoweth unto whom I shall, as I am most bounded, incessantly pray for the countenance and prosperous conservation of your most excellent, most royal and imperial estate long to endure.

ii. Gresham's Proposals at the accession of Elizabeth I

It was largely through Gresham's work that the Elizabethan reign was established on such a sound financial footing.

Source: J. W. Burgon, *Life and Times of Sir Thomas Gresham* (1839) i. p. 486

Finally, and it please your Majesty to restore this your realm into such estate, as heretofore it hath been; first, your Highness hath none other ways, but when time and opportunity serveth, to bring your brass money into fine of 11 ounces fine, and so gold after the rate.

Secondly, not to restore the Steelyard to their usurped privileges.

Thirdly, to grant as few licences as you can.

Fourthly, to come in as small debt as you can beyond seas.

Fifthly, to keep [up] your credit, and especially with your own merchants, for it is they must stand by you at all events in your necessity. And thus I shall most humbly beseech your Majesty to accept this my [poor writing in good] part; wherein I shall from time to time, as opportunity doth serve, put your Highness in remembrance, according to the trust your Majesty hath reposed in me; beseeching the Lord to give me the grace and fortune that my service may always be acceptable to your Highness: as knoweth our Lord, whom preserve your noble Majesty in health, and long to reign over us with increase of honour.

> By your Majesty's most humble and
> faithful obedient subject,

> THOMAS GRESHAM, Mercer

iii. *William Cecil's Industrial and Social Programme,* 1559

Source: Hist. MSS. Comm. MSS. of the Marquis of Salisbury pt. i. pp. 162–3

Considerations delivered to the Parliament, 1559

I. *Vagabonds.* That the Statute 1 Edward VI, Chap. 8, concerning idle persons and vagabonds being made slaves, now repealed, be revived with additions.

II. *Labourers and Servants.* That the Statutes 12 Richard II, Chap. 3, 'that no servant or labourer at the end of this term depart out of the hundred or place where he dwells,' etc., and 13 Richard II, Chap. 7, ordering the Justices at every session to appoint by proclamation the wages of workers, etc., be confirmed with the addition: 'that no man hereafter receive into service any servant without a testimonial from the master he last dwelt with, sealed with a Parish Seal kept by the constable or churchwarden, witnessing he left with the free licence of his master, penalty £10.' So, by the hands of the masters, servants may be reduced to obedience, which shall reduce obedience to the Prince and to God also; by the looseness of the time no other remedy is left but by awe of law to acquaint men with virtue again, whereby the reformation of religion may be brought in credit, with the amendment of manners, the want whereof has been imputed as a thing grown by the liberty of the gospel, etc.

III. *Husbandry.* That the Statutes, 4 Henry VII, Chap. 9, 'for re-edifying houses of husbandry, and to avoid the decay of towns and villages,' and 5 Edward VI, Chap. 5, 'for maintenance of husbandry and tillage', be put in execution.

IV. *Purchase of Lands.* No husbandman, yeoman or artificer to purchase above £5 by the year of inheritance, save in cities, towns and boroughs, for their better repair; one mansion house only to be purchased over and above the said yearly value. The common purchasing thereof is the ground of dearth of victuals, raising of rents, etc.

V. *Merchants.* No merchant to purchase above £50 a year of inheritance, except aldermen and sheriffs of London, who, because they approach to the degree of knighthood, may purchase to the value of £200.

VI. *Apprentices.* None to be received apprentice except his father may spend 40s. a year of freehold, nor to be apprenticed to a merchant except his father spend £10 a year of freehold or be descended from a gentleman or merchant. Through the idleness of these professions so many embrace them that they are only a cloak for vagabonds and thieves, and there is such a decay of husbandry that masters cannot get skilful servants to till the ground without unreasonable wages, etc.

iv. The Statute of Apprentices, 1563

Source: Statutes of the Realm, iv. I. pp. 414–17, 419–21

I. Although there remain and stand in force presently a great number of Acts and Statutes concerning . . . apprentices servants and labourers . . . [yet] the said laws cannot conveniently . . . be put in . . . execution and . . . if the substance of as many of the said laws as are meet to be continued shall be digested and reduced into one sole law and Statute, and in the same an uniform order prescribed and limited concerning the wages and other orders . . . there is good hope that . . . the same law . . . should banish idleness, advance husbandry and yield unto the hired person both in the time of scarcity and in the time of plenty a convenient proportion of wages: Be it therefore enacted. . . .

II. That no manner of person [after 30th Sept. next] . . . shall be retained hired or taken into service . . . to work for any less . . . term than for one holy year, in any of the sciences . . . or arts of clothiers . . . shoemakers . . . pewterers, bakers, brewers . . . saddlers [&c.] . . .

XI. That the Justices of Peace of every shire . . . shall have authority by virtue hereof, within the limits . . . of their several commissions to . . . rate and appoint the wages [of all labourers, artificers, &c.] . . .

XXIV. That after [1 May next], it shall not be lawful to any person . . . other than such as now do lawfully . . . exercise any art . . . to set up . . . any craft . . . except he shall have been brought up therein seven years at the least . . . in manner and form above said, nor to set any person on work in such mystery . . . being not a workman at this day, except he shall have been apprentice as is aforesaid, or else having served as an apprentice . . . will become a journeyman. . . .

XXX. That the Justices of Peace of every county . . . shall yearly . . . make a special and diligent enquiry of the branches and articles of this Statute . . . and where they shall find any defaults, to see the same severely corrected and punished.

Source: W. J. Hardy, *Hertford Session Rolls, 1581–1698* (1906), quoted in Wernham & Walker, *England under Elizabeth* (1932) p. 215

Reaping, binding and laying of wheat or rye in shocks[1] well grown and not ledged by the acre   iid. . . .

Labourers from the Annunciation of our Lady until Michaelmas not to have more by the day than with meat and drink   iiid. . . .

And without [meat and drink]   viiid. . . .

Masons, carpenters, joiners, wheelwrights, ploughwrights, bricklayers, tilers, and plasterers, being masters of the said occupations, or of the best sort shall not have more by the day than with meat and drink   viiid. . . .

The same of the second sort shall not take more by the day than with meat and drink   vid. . . .

A man servant [of husbandry] of the best sort shall not have more by the year than with a livery   xls. . . .

The best sort of women servants shall not have more by the year than with a livery   xxis. . . .

A shoemaker servant of the best sort being married to have without meat and drink for every dozen of shoes   xxiid. . . .

vi. Poor Relief

Two clear problems were involved here, the relief of the deserving poor, and the punishment of vagrants and idlers. The distinction was made clear in the Statute of 1531; and, as usual under the Tudors, the administration of these problems was delegated to the Justices of the Peace.

(a) Beggars Act of 1531

Source: Statutes of the Realm, iii. p. 328

I. Where in all places . . . vagabonds and beggars have of long time increased . . . in great and excessive numbers, by the occasion of idleness, mother and root of all vices. . . . Be it therefore enacted

---

[1] East Anglian for stooks.

... That the Justices of the Peace ... shall make diligent search and enquiry of all aged, poor, and impotent persons which live or of necessity be compelled to live by alms of the charity of the people that be or shall be hereafter abiding ... within the limits of their division, and after ... such search made the said Justices of Peace ... shall have power ... to enable to beg ... such of the said impotent persons which they shall find and think most convenient within the limits of their division ... [and] that none of them shall beg without the limits to them so appointed, and shall also register and write the names of every such impotent beggar [by them appointed] in a bill or roll indented, the one part thereof to remain with themselves and the other part by them to be certified before the Justices of Peace ... the said Justices ... shall make ... a letter containing the name of such impotent person and witnessing that he is authorised to beg. ... And if any such impotent person so authorised to beg do beg in any other place than within such limits ... the Justices of Peace ... shall ... punish all such persons by imprisonment in the stocks by the space of 2 days and 2 nights, giving them but only bread and water. ...

III. ... That if any person or persons being whole and mighty in body and able to labour ... be vagrant ... that then it shall be lawful to the constables and all other the King's officers ... to arrest the said vagabonds ... and them to bring to any of the Justices of Peace ... and that every such Justice of Peace ... shall cause every such idle person so to him brought to be had to the next market town or other place ... and there to be tied to the end of a cart naked and be beaten with whips throughout the same market town or other place till his body be bloody by reason of such whipping and after such punishment ... the person so punished ... shall be enjoined upon his oath to return forthwith without delay in the next and straight way to the place where he was born, or where he last dwelled before the same punishment by the space of 3 years, and there put himself to labour like as a true man oweth to do ... [and] every such person so punished ... shall have a letter ... witnessing that he hath been punished according to this Estatute. ... And if he do not accomplish the order to him appointed by the said letter, then to be eftsoons[1] taken and whipped. ...

[1] a second time.

And that the Justices of the Peace . . . shall have power . . . to enquire of all mayors, bailiffs, constables, and other officers and persons that shall be negligent in executing of this Act.

(b) The organization of poor relief is shown by the Statute of 1598

Source: Statutes of the Realm, iv. 2. pp. 896–8

I. Be it enacted . . . that the churchwardens of every parish, and four substantial householders there . . . who shall be nominated yearly in Easter Week, under the hand and seal of two or more Justices of the Peace in the same county . . . shall be called Overseers of the poor of the same parishes: and they . . . shall take order from time to time . . . with the consent of two or more such Justices of Peace for setting to work of the children of all such whose parents shall not by the said persons be thought able to keep and maintain their children. And also all such persons married or unmarried as having no means to maintain them, use no ordinary and daily trade of life to get their living by; and also to raise weekly or otherwise . . . a convenient stock of flax . . . and other necessary ware and stuff to set the poor on work, and also competent sums of money for . . . the necessary relief of the lame impotent old blind and such other among them being poor and not able to work, and also for the putting out of such children to be apprentices . . . and to do . . . all other things . . . concerning the premises, as to them shall seem convenient. . . .

II. That if the said Justices of Peace do perceive that the inhabitants of any parish are not able to levy among themselves sufficient sums of money . . . that then [they] shall and may . . . assess as aforesaid any other of other parishes . . . within the Hundred. . . . And if the said Hundred shall not be thought to [them] able and fit [so] to relieve . . . then the Justices of Peace at their general Quarter Sessions. . . shall rate . . . any other of other parishes . . . within the said County. . . .

III. And that it shall be lawful for the said . . . Overseers . . . by warrant from any such two Justices of Peace to levy . . . the said sums of money of every one that shall refuse to contribute . . . by distraint and sale of the offender's goods . . . and in defect of such distraint it shall be lawful for any such two Justices of the Peace to commit him to prison, there to remain . . . till payment of the said sum. . . .

XII. And forasmuch as all begging is forbidden by this present Act . . . the Justices of Peace . . . shall rate every parish to such a weekly sum of money as they shall think convenient . . . which sums so taxed shall be yearly assessed by the agreement of the parishioners within themselves.

vii. The Encouragement of Industry

One of the most important aspects of what might be called the Government's economic programme was the encouragement of national self-sufficiency. In particular, mining was supported with a view to the development of armament-manufacture; this expanded considerably during the reign, as did many other kinds of industry.

Source: Patent Rolls 10 *Eliz.*, Part v, printed by the Selden Society, vol. 28. pp. 4–15

Elizabeth by the grace of God, &c. To all unto whom these presents come, greeting.

Whereas we . . . have . . . given and granted full power, licence and authority to Thomas Thurland, clerk . . . and to Daniel Houghsetter, a German born . . . to search . . . for all manner of monies or ores of gold, silver, copper, or quicksilver, within our counties of York, Lancaster, Cumberland, Westmoreland, Cornwall, Devon, Gloucestershire, and Worcestershire, and within our principality of Wales, or in any of them, and the same to try out, convert, and use to their most profit and commodity. . . .

And whereas our pleasure, intent, and meaning in our said Letters Patent was that, for the better help and more commodity of the said Thomas Thurland and Daniel Houghsetter and their several assignees, they . . . might . . . grant . . . parts and portions of the said licences . . . and thereupon their several assignees have . . . granted . . . to . . . William, Earl of Pembroke, and Robert, Earl of Leicestershire, and to . . . James, Lord Mountjoy, and to Sir William Cecil, knight, our principal secretary, and John

Tamworth and John Dudley, esquires, Leonell Duchet, citizen and alderman of London, Benedict Spynola, of London, merchant, John Lover, William Winter, Anthony Duckett, of the county of Westmoreland, gentlemen . . . Daniel Ulstett, a German born, [and ten others] divers parts and portions of the licences, powers, authorities, privileges, benefits and immunities aforesaid.

By force whereof the said Thomas Thurland and Daniel Houghsetter . . . have travailed in the search, work and experiment of the mines and ores aforesaid . . . and have now brought the said work to very good effect, whereby great benefit is like to come to us and this our realm of England, which also will the rather come to pass if the persons . . . having interest in the privileges aforesaid might by our grant be incorporated and made a perpetual body politic. . . .

Know ye, therefore, that we . . . do give and grant to the afore-named William Earl of Pembroke [and the others as above] that they by the name of Governor, Assistants, and Commonalty for the Mines Royal shall be from henceforth one body politic in itself incorporate, and a perpetual society of themselves both in deed and name. . . .

And further, we . . . will grant . . . that they . . . shall and may not only admit into the said corporation and society such and as many persons as by the statutes . . . shall be prescribed . . . so that every such person . . . shall . . . have for the term of his life at the least the benefit of a quarter of one four-and-twenty part of the licenses, powers, authorities, privileges, benefits and communities aforesaid . . . but also shall and may minister to every such person to be admitted an oath tending to the due performing and keeping of the rules, statutes, and ordinances in form aforesaid to be made.

The Justices of the Peace

i. An Elizabethan Commission of the Peace

> *Source:* W. Lambard, *Eirenarcha* (ed. 1614) pp. 35–8

Elizabeth by the grace of God, &c. . . . Know that we have assigned you, jointly and severally, and each of you, to be our Justices to keep our peace in our county of . . . and to keep and cause to be kept all ordinances and statutes published for the good of our peace and for the keeping thereof and for the quiet rule and government of our people . . . as well within liberties as without. . . .

Further we assign you . . . (of whom we will you, A. B. C. D. &c., to be one) . . . to inquire by oath of good and lawful men of the county . . . of all and every felonies, poisonings, enchantments, sorceries, arts magic, trespasses, forestallings, regratings, engrossings and extortions whatsoever, and all other crimes and offences (of which our Justices of the Peace can or ought lawfully to inquire) . . . and of such as go or ride armed in assemblies against our peace in disturbance of our people . . . and of such as lie in wait to maim or kill our people; and of innkeepers and all others who in weights and measures or in selling of victuals offend against the ordinances and statutes published for the common weal of our realm of England and of our people . . . and of such sheriffs, bailiffs, stewards, constables, keepers of gaols and other officers as are lukewarm, remiss or negligent in the performance of their offices. . . .

And to hear and determine all and singular the felonies . . . and the rest of the premisses . . . and to correct and punish the same offenders for their crimes by fines, ransoms, amercements, forfeitures and otherwise. . . .

ii. The Justices at Work, 1597–8

> *Source:* J. Lister, *West Riding Sessions Rolls, 1598–1602* (Yorkshire Arch. Assoc., 1888) pp. 27, 40–1, 59–60, 104, 130, 133, 142–3

For that information is given unto this Court by the High Constables of Staincross that Adam Hutchonson and Thomas Hodgson of Barnsley alehousekeepers are men of bad behaviour and do maintain ill rule in their houses. It is therefore ordered that a warrant *per curiam* shall be made against them to discharge them for keeping any alehouses . . . until reformation be had &c. . . .

Whereas there is a poor infant child left within the town of Southerham, who are so sore charged with their own poor that they are scarce able to relieve them and therefore hath required aid of this Court. It is therefore ordered that the said child shall not only be relieved within the same town . . . but also through the whole parish of Halifax until other order be therein taken. . . .

Ordered that no brewsters within this division shall brew any ale or beer of greater price to be sold or sell any for any greater price than only of a penny the quart, except they shall have a special licence from some Justice of Peace. . . .

It is also ordered that all persons restrained for buying corn or malting shall stand so restrained until the next Sessions, because we have received some direction for these special causes and therefore purpose to have a special Sessions. . . .

Whereas the highway leading from Leeds to Wikebrigg . . . hath been heretofore presented by jury to be in great decay . . . to the great hindrance of all her Majesty's subjects that have occasion to travel that way. Therefore the foresaid jurors by the consent of the Justices here present, do lay a pain that every person occupying a plough tilth of land within any the parishes of Leeds . . . shall send their draughts and sufficient labourers according to the Statute [29 Eliz., c.5.], and repair the same way before [Aug. 25] upon pain . . . [of] xxs. . . .

Forasmuch as Thomas Stringar was brought here in Court for suspicion of sheep stealing and did confess himself guilty thereof: it is therefore ordered that he shall be conveyed to Wenbridge from whence he came and there by the Constable whipped being stripped naked from the middle upwards. . . .

[The jurors say that] John Tottie of Wakefield clothier being appointed one of the searchers of Wakefield . . . did alter the assize of his tentor[1], and made the chase thereof bigger then was

[1] Device for stretching cloth.

agreed and set down by him and the residue of the searchers. . . .

Forasmuch as this Court is credibly informed that one Thomas Hargraves an underbailiff and William Longcaster a promoter, hath committed sundry misdemeanours, the one in summoning diverse freeholders to the Assizes and Sessions and after taking money of them for their discharge, the other in suing diverse her Majesty's subjects and afterwards . . . making unlawful compositions with them: it is therefore ordered that an attachment *per curiam* shall be made against them to answer their several offences at the next Sessions and in the mean time to be of good behaviour.

❖

Trade

i. Henry VII's Treaties with the Netherlands

Source: Bacon, *History of King Henry VII*, 1621 (ed. Lumby) p. 145

By this time, being the eleventh year of the King, the interruption of trade between the English and the Flemish began to pinch the merchants of both nations very sore: which moved them by all means they could devise, to effect and dispose their sovereigns respectively, to open the intercourse again; wherein time favoured them. For the Archduke and his council began to see, that Perkin would prove but a runagate and citizen of the world and that it was the part of children to fall out about babies. And the King on his part, after the attempts upon Kent and Northumberland, began to have the business of Perkin in less estimation; so as he did not put it to account in any consultation of state. But that which moved him most was, that being a King that loved wealth and treasure, he could not endure to have trade sick, nor any obstruction to continue in the gatevein, which disperseth that blood. And yet he kept state so far, as first to be sought unto. Wherein the merchant-adventurers likewise, being a strong company at that time, and well under-set with rich men, and good order, did hold out bravely; taking off the commodities of the kingdom, though they lay dead upon their hands for want of vent. At the last, commissioners met at London to treat. These concluded a perfect treaty, both of amity and intercourse, between the King and the Archduke, containing articles both of state, commerce and free fishing. This is that treaty which the Flemings call at this day *Intercursus magnus*; both because it is more complete than the precedent treaties of the third and fourth year of the King, and chiefly to give it a difference from the treaty that followed in the one and twentieth year of the King, which they call *Intercursus malus*. In this treaty there was an express article against the reception of the rebels of either prince by other. But nevertheless in this article Perkin was not named, neither perhaps contained, because he was no rebel. But by this means his wings were clipped of his followers that were English. And it was expressly comprised in the treaty, that it should extend to the territories of the duchess dowager. After the intercourse thus restored, the English merchants came again to their mansion at Antwerp, where they were received with procession and great joy.

ii. *Privileges obtained by Anthony Jenkinson from the Emperor of Russia, 22 September, 1567*

Source: Hakluyt, *Principal Navigations*, iii. p. 95

We have granted them to buy and sell in all our kingdoms and castles, with all kind of wares: and we have also licensed them, that when those English merchants do desire to buy and sell with our merchants wholly together, that they shall have liberty so to do wholly together: and they that do desire to sell their own wares by retail in their own house, that then they sell it in their own house by retail to our people and other strangers, as they can agree: and weights and arshnids[1] to be kept in their house with our seal, and they themselves to barter and sell their own wares: and no Russian merchant in Moscow, or any other place in our kingdom to sell

[1] Russian measure of length.

them any wares, nor to buy or barter any wares for them, nor [sell] any strangers' goods.

iii. The Spanish Ambassador, Mendoza, to Philip II, 15 May 1582

Source: Cal. S. P. Spanish, iii. pp. 366–7

The English also settled through the Muscovite with the Tartars on the banks of the Volga to allow the free passage of their merchandise down the river to the Caspian Sea; whilst the Persian . . . should give them leave to trade and distribute their merchandise, through Media and Persia, in exchange for goods which reach the Persians by the rivers that run from the East Indies to the Caspian Sea. This privilege was granted. . . .

Two years ago they opened up the trade, which they still continue, to the Levant, which is extremely profitable to them, as they take great quantities of tin and lead thither. . . . In order to carry on the trade with more safety and speed . . . [they] requested permission of the Turk to go from Azov by the Don and Port Euxine and sell their goods from Media and Persia by the Caspian Sea and the river Volga to the river Don, the distance between the two rivers at one point not being more than a German league. . . . A depot was thus to be formed to concentrate the trade of the two rivers . . . and to serve as a point of distribution for goods brought from England, for . . . the whole of the Levant, without their having to pass, as at present, by Italy.

iv. The Charter to the East India Company, 31 December 1600

Source: G. Birdwood & W. Foster, First Letter Book of the East India Company (1893) pp. 163–84

Elizabeth by the grace of God [etc.] whereas . . . George, Earl of Cumberland [and 217 others] have . . . been petitioners unto us . . . that they . . . might adventure and set forth one or more voyages with convenient number of ships and pinnaces . . . to the East Indies. . . .

II. Know ye therefore that we . . . do give and grant to our loving subjects . . . that they . . . be a body corporate and politic in deed and in name by the name of the Governor and Company of merchants of London trading into the East Indies. . . . And that . . . they shall have succession . . . [and be] capable in law. . . .

V. And . . . we do ordain that there shall be from henceforth one of the same Company elected . . . which shall be called the Governor . . . and that there shall be . . . twenty four . . . elected . . . which shall be called the Committees [who together with the Governor] . . . shall have the direction of the voyages of or for the said Company and the provision of the shipping and merchandizes thereto belonging, and also the sale of all merchandizes returned in the voyages . . . and the managing and handling of all other things belonging to the said Company. . . .

VII. And . . . they or the greater part of them, whereof the Governor . . . or his Deputy to be one . . . shall . . . yearly . . . meet together . . . to elect . . . one of the said Company, which shall be Governor . . . for one whole year [who shall take an oath before entering on office]. . . .

XII. And . . . they . . . and all the sons of them . . . at their several ages of twenty-one years . . . and further all such the apprentices factors or servants . . . of them, which hereafter shall be employed . . . may by the space of 15 years . . . freely traffic and use the trade of merchandize by seas in and by such ways and passages . . . as they shall . . . take to be fittest into and from the said East Indies into the countries and parts of Asia and Africa and into and from all the islands . . . and places of Asia Africa and America . . . beyond the Cape of Bona Esperanza to the straits of Magellan . . . in such order . . . as shall be . . . at any . . . Court held by or for the said Governor . . . limited and agreed: and not otherwise. . . .

XIII. [Power to make laws and ordinances, and to punish offenders either in body or purse, the said laws and punishments not being contrary to the laws of the realm.]

XXII. . . . By virtue of our prerogative royal . . . we straight charge . . . all the subjects of us . . . that none of them directly or indirectly visit . . . or trade . . . [into] the said East Indies . . . or places aforesaid other then the said Governor . . . unless it be by . . . licence and agreement of the said Governor . . . [upon pain of forfeiture of goods and ships].

❖

The Voyages

i. Cabot

A letter from Lorenzo Pasqualigo to his brothers at Venice, 23 August, 1497.

Source: Cal. S. P. Venetian i. p. 262

London, 23rd August, 1497

Our Venetian, who went with a small ship from Bristol to find new islands, has come back, and says he has discovered, seven hundred leagues off, the mainland of the country of the Great Khan and that he coasted along it for 300 leagues, and landed, but did not see any person. But he has brought here to the King certain snares spread to take game, and a needle for making nets; and he found some notched trees, from which he judged that there were inhabitants. Being in doubt, he came back to the ship. He has been away three months on the voyage, which is certain, and in returning he saw two islands to the right, but he did not wish to land, lest he should lose time, for he was in want of provisions. This King has been much pleased. He says that the tides are slack, and do not make currents as they do here. The King has promised for another time, ten armed ships as he desires, and has given him all the prisoners, except such as are confined for high treason, to go with him, as he has requested; and has granted him money to amuse himself till then. Meanwhile he is with his Venetian wife and his sons at Bristol. His name is Zuam Cabot and he is called the Great Admiral, great honour being paid to him, and he goes dressed in silk. The English are ready to go with him, and so are many of our rascals. The discoverer of these things has planted a large cross in the ground with a banner of England, and one of St Mark, as he is a Venetian; so that our flag has been hoisted very far away.

ii. Drake's Circumnavigation

He takes possession of what is now California.

Source: Sir F. Drake, *The World Encompassed* (Hakluyt Society Series 1. No. 16, 1854) pp. 114, 132

In 38 deg. 30 mins, we fell with a convenient and fit harbour and June 17 came to anchor therein, where we continued till the 23 day of July following. . . .

This country our General named Albion, and that for two causes; the one in respect of the white banks and cliffs, which lie toward the sea; the other that it might have some affinity, even in name also, with our own country, which was sometime so called.

Before we went from thence, our General caused to be set up a monument of our being there, as also of her Majesty's and successors' right and title to that kingdom; namely a plate of brass, fast nailed to a great and firm post; whereon is engraven her Grace's name, and the day and year of our arrival there, and of the free giving up of the province and kingdom, both by the King and people, into her Majesty's hands: together with her Highness' picture and arms, in a piece of sixpence current English money, showing itself by a hole made of purpose through the plate; underneath was likewise engraven the name of our General, etc.

iii. Early Virginia

A letter from Ralph Lane, Governor of Virginia 1585–7, giving a picture not borne out by pioneers in the early days of the colony.

Source: Hakluyt, *Principal Navigations* viii. pp. 318–20

In the meanwhile you shall understand, that since Sir Richard Grenville's departure from us, as also before, we have discovered the main to be the goodliest oil under the cope of heaven, so abounding with sweet trees, that bring such sundry rich and pleasant gums, grapes of such greatness, yet wild, as France, Spain nor Italy have no greater, so many sorts of apothecary drugs, such several kinds of flax, and one kind like silk, the same gathered of a grass, as common there, as grass is here. And now within these few days we have found here maize or Guinea wheat, whose ear yieldeth corn for bread 400, upon one ear, and the cane maketh very good and perfect sugar, also *Terra Samia*, otherwise *Terra sigillata*. Besides that, it is the goodliest and most pleasing territory of the world: for the continent is of an huge unknown greatness, and very well peopled and towned, though savagely, and the climate so wholesome, that we had not one sick since we touched the land here. To conclude, if Virginia had but horses and kine in some reasonable proportion, I dare assure myself being inhabited with English, no realm in Christendom were comparable to it. For this already we find, that what commodities soever Spain, France, Italy or the East parts so yield unto us, in wines of all sorts, in oils, in flax, in resins, pitch, frankincense, currants, sugars, and such like, these parts do abound with the growth of them all, but being savages that possess the land, they know no use of the same. And sundry other rich commodities, that no parts of the world, be they West or East Indies, have, here we find great abundance of. The people naturally are most courteous, and very desirous to have clothes, but especially of coarse cloth rather than silk, coarse canvas they also like well of, but copper carrieth the price of all, so it be made red. Thus good M. Hakluyt and M. H., I have joined you both in one letter of remembrance, as two that I love dearly well, and commending me most heartily to you both, I commit you to the tuition of the Almighty. From the new fort in Virginia, this third of September, 1585.

Your most assured friend Ralph Lane.

❖

A Foreign View of England

Source: Venetian Relation, c. 1498 (translated for the Camden Society) p. 20

The English are, for the most part, both men and women of all ages, handsome and well-proportioned; though not quite so much so, in my opinion, as it had been asserted to me, before your Magnificence went to that kingdom; and I have understood from persons acquainted with these countries that the Scotch are much handsomer; and that the English are great lovers of themselves, and of everything belonging to them; they think that there are no other men than themselves, and no other world but England: and whenever they see a handsome foreigner, they say that 'he looks like an Englishman', and that 'it is a great pity that he should not be an Englishman'; and when they partake of any delicacy with a foreigner, they ask him, 'whether such a thing is made in their country?' They take great pleasure in having a quantity of excellent victuals, and also in remaining a long time at table, being very sparing of wine when they drink it at their own expense . . . and they think that no greater honour can be conferred or received than to invite others to eat with them, or to be invited themselves; and they would sooner give five or six ducats to provide an entertainment for a person, than a groat to assist him in any distress.

They all from time immemorial wear very fine clothes, and are extremely polite in their language; which, although it is as well as the Flemish derived from the German, has lost its natural harshness, and is pleasing enough as they pronounce it. In addition to their civil speeches, they have the incredible courtesy of remaining with their heads uncovered with an admirable grace, whilst they talk to each other. They are gifted with good understandings, and are very quick at everything they apply their minds to; few, however, excepting the clergy, are addicted to the study of letters; and this is the reason why anyone who has learning, though he may be a layman, is called by them a clerk. And yet they have great advantages for study, there being two general universities in the kingdom, Oxford and Cambridge; in which are many colleges founded for the maintenance of poor scholars. And your Magnificence lodged at one named Magdalen, in the University of Oxford, of which the founders have been prelates, so the scholars are also ecclesiastics.

The common people apply themselves to trade, or to fishing, or else they practise navigation; and they are so diligent in mercantile pursuits, that they do not fear to make contracts on usury.

Although they all attend mass every day, and say many Paternosters in public (the women carrying long rosaries in their hands, and any who can read taking the office of Our Lady with them, and with some companion reciting it in the church verse by verse, in a low voice, after the manner of churchmen), they always hear mass on Sunday in their parish church, and give liberal alms, because they may not offer less than a piece of money of which fourteen are equivalent to a golden ducat; nor do they omit any form incumbent upon good Christians; there are, however, many who have various opinions concerning religion.

They have a very high reputation in arms; and from the great fear the French entertain of them, one must believe it to be justly acquired. But I have it on the best information, that when the war is raging most furiously, they will seek for good eating, and all their other comforts, without thinking of what harm might befall them. . . .

The want of affection in the English is strongly manifested towards their children; for after having kept them at home till they arrive at the age of seven or nine years at the utmost, they put them out, both males and females, to hard service in the houses of other people, binding them generally for another seven or nine years. And these are called apprentices, and during that time they perform all the most menial offices; and few are born who are exempted from this fate, for every one, however rich he may be, sends away his children into the houses of others whilst he, in return, receives those of strangers into his own. And on inquiring their reason for this severity, they answered that they did it in order that their children might learn better manners. But I, for my part, believe

138

that they do it because they like to enjoy all their comforts themselves, and that they are better served by strangers than they would
be by their own children. Besides which the English being great
epicures, and very avaricious by nature, indulge in the most delicate
fare themselves and give their household the coarsest bread, and
beer, and cold meat baked on Sunday for the week, which, however,
they allow them in great abundance.

◆

Education

i. The New Learning in England

Source: *Epistles of Erasmus* (ed. F. M. Nichols 1901) i. p. 225

Erasmus to Robert Fisher

I am a little afraid of writing to you, my dear Robert; not because I fear that your affection for me has been at all impaired by
this great separation in time and space, but because you are now
in that part of the world where the very walls are more learned
and scholarly than the men are with us; so that what we think here,
fine, exquisite, tasteful, charming, cannot help seeming there,
crude, poor and insipid. So you must understand that England
expects to find you not only an expert jurist but also equally
loquacious in Latin and Greek. And you would long ago have seen
me with you, had not my Lord Mountjoy carried me off to his
native England, when I was ready for the journey. And, indeed,
where would I not follow a gentleman of such refinement, kindness,
and affability? Nay, upon my word, I would follow him to the
world's end. . . . But, you ask, how do you like our England? If
you trust me at all, Robert, I assure you that I have never liked
anything so much in all my life. I have found here a climate as

pleasant as it is healthy; no end of kindness; and so much real learning, not commonplace and paltry, but profound accurate ancient Latin and Greek, that, save for the satisfaction of seeing it, I do not now so much care of Italy. When I am listening to my friend Colet, I seem to be listening to Plato himself. In Grocyn who does not marvel at such a perfection of learning? What can be more acute, profound, and delicate than the judgment of Linacre? What has Nature ever created more gentle, more sweet, more happy than the genius of Thomas More? I need go no further. It is wonderful how widespread and abundant is the harvest of ancient learning in this country—to which you should therefore all the sooner return. . . . Farewell.

From London in haste, this fifth day of December.

ii. *The methods of the time*

A letter to Thomas Cromwell from the tutor of his son, Gregory.

Source: Ellis, *Original Letters, Third Series*, i. pp. 342–3

After that it pleased your mastership to give me in charge, not only to give diligent attendance upon Master Gregory, but also to instruct him with good letters, honest manners, pastime of instruments, and such other qualities as it should be for him meet and convenient, pleaseth it you to understand that for the accomplishment thereof I have endeavoured myself by all ways possible to excogitate how I might most profit him. In which behalf, through his diligence, the success is such as I trust shall be to your good contentation and pleasure, and to his no small profit. But for cause the summer was spent in the service of the wild gods, [and] it is so much to be regarded after what fashion youth is brought up, in which time that that is learned for the most part will not be wholly forgotten in the older years, I think it my duty to ascertain your mastership how he spendeth his time. And first after he hath heard Mass he taketh a lecture of a dialogue of Erasmus' *Colloquies*, called *Pietas Pueribus*, wherein is described a very picture of one that should be virtuously brought up; and for cause it is so necessary for him, I do not only cause him to read it over, but also to practise the precepts of the same. After this he exerciseth his hand in writing one or two hours, and readeth upon Fabyan's *Chronicle* as long. The residue of the day he doth spend upon the lute and virginals. When he rideth, as he doth very oft, I tell him by the way some history of the Romans or the Greeks, which I cause him to rehearse again in a tale. For his recreation he useth to hawk and hunt and shoot in his long bow, which frameth and succeedeth so well with him that he seemeth to be thereunto given by nature.

iii. *Richard Mulcaster, a Tudor Schoolmaster*

Source: Thomas Fuller, *The Worthies of England* (1662) p. 139

Richard Mulcaster was born [1530?] of an ancient extract in the north; but whether in this county [Westmorland] or Cumberland, I find not decided. From Eton school he went to Cambridge, where he was admitted into King's College, 1548; but, before he graduated, removed to Oxford. Here such was his proficiency in learning, that by general consent he was chosen the first master of Merchant Taylors' School in London, which prospered well under his care, as, by the flourishing of Saint John's in Oxford, doth plainly appear.

The Merchant Taylors, finding his scholars so to profit, intended to fix Mr Mulcaster at his desk to their school, till death should remove him. This he perceived, and therefore gave for his motto, *Fidelis servus, perpetuus asinus*. But after twenty-five years he procured his freedom, or rather exchanged his service, being made Master of St Paul's School.

His method of teaching was this. In a morning he would exactly and plainly construe and parse the lessons to his scholars; which done, he slept his hour (custom made him critical to proportion it) in his desk in the school; but woe be to the scholar that slept the while. Awaking, he heard them accurately; and Atropos might be persuaded to pity, as soon as he to pardon, where he found just fault. The prayers of cockering mothers prevailed with him as much as the requests of indulgent fathers, rather increasing than mitigating his severity on their offending child.

In a word he was *plagosus Orbilius*; though it may be truly said (and safely for one out of his school) that others have taught as much learning with fewer lashes. Yet his sharpness was the better endured, because unpartial; and many excellent scholars were bred under him, whereof Bishop Andrewes was most remarkable.

Then quitting that place, he was presented to the rich parsonage of Stanford Rivers in Essex. I have heard from those who have heard him preach, that his sermons were not excellent, which to me seems no wonder: partly because there is a different discipline in teaching children and men; partly because such who make divinity not the choice of their youth, but the refuge of their age, seldom attain to eminency therein.

❖

The Sweating Sickness

Plagues were still a normal occurrence in sixteenth-century England, a fact which is often overlooked by those who remember only the big outbreaks—the Black Death and the Plague of 1665. Rich people could leave the insanitary towns during outbreaks but, even so, they were far from immune.

Source: Edward Hall, *Life of Henry VIII* (ed. Whibley, 1904) ii. p. 137

In the very end of May began in the city of London the sickness called the sweating sickness, and afterward went all the realm almost of the which many died within 5 or 6 hours. By reason of this sickness the term was adjourned and the circuits of Assize also. The King was sore troubled with this plague, for divers died in the Court, of whom one was Sir Frances Poynes which was Ambassador in Spain, and other, so that the King for a space removed almost every day, till at the last he came to Tittenhangar a place of the Abbot of St Alban's and there he with a few determined to bide the chance that God would send him, which place was so purged daily with fires and other preservatives, that neither he nor the Queen nor none of their company was infected with that disease, such was the pleasure of God. In this great plague died Sir William Compton knight and William Cary esquire which were of the King's privy chamber, and whom the King highly favoured and many other worshipful men and women in England.

❖

Appendix

1. *Funeral sermon preached by Bishop Fisher 10 May 1509, on the death of Henry VII* (see page 19)

his polytyque wysedome in gouernaunce it was synguler, his wytte alway quycke and redy, his reason pyththy and substancyall, his memory fresshe and holdynge, his experyence notable, his counseylles fortunate and taken by wyse delyberacyon, his speche gracyous in dyuerse languages, his persone goodly and amyable, his naturall compleccyon of the purest myxture, his yssue fayre and in good nombre, leages and confyderyes he hadde with all crysten prynces, his mighty power was dredde euery where, not onely within his realme but without also, his people were to hym in as humble subgeccyon as euer they were to kynge, his londe many a day in peas and tranquyllyte, his prosperyte in batayle ayenst his enemyes was meruaylous, his delynge in tyme of perylles and daungers was colde and sobre with grete hardynesse. If ony treason were conspyred ayenst hym it came out wonderfully, his treasour and rychesse incomparable, his buyldynges mooste goodly and after the newest cast all of pleasure. But what is all this now as vnto hym, all be but *Fumus & vmbra*. A smoke that soone vanyssheth, and a shadowe soone passynge awaye.

2. *Edward VI's devise for the succession, May 1553* (see page 66 and Plate 32)

My devise for the Succession.
For Lakke of issu of my body To the L Franceses heires masles, if she have any such issu befor my death to the L Jane and her heires masles, To the L Katerins heires masles, To the L Maries

144

heires masles, To the heires masles of the daughters wich she shal have hereafter then to the L Margets heires masles. For lakke of such issu, To theires masles of the L Janes daughters To theires masles of the L Katerins daughters and so forth til you come to the L Margets daughters heires masles.

2. If after my death theire masle be entred into 18 yere old, then he to have the hole rule and gouuernance thereof.

3. But if he be under 18, then his mother to be gouuernes til he entre 18 yere old But to doe nothing wout the'avise and agrement of 6 parcel of a counsel to be pointed by my last will to the nombre of 20.

4. If the mother die befor theire entre into 18 the realme to be gouuerned by the cousel [sic] Provided that after he be 14 yere al great matters of importaunce be opened to him.

3. *Gresham to Parry, Antwerp, 16 June 1560* (see page 84)

Here Majestie now neaddythe not to have anny kynde of fere of the Frenche King or the King of Spayen for anny dommage the can do to Here Hightnes anny manner of wayes. . . . As licke wysee, where as Here Majestie owythe one myllyone of dockats. I am right assewrid that King Phillipe and the Frenche King owith eche of them a pece xx millions, so, that all thinges consideryd, Here Ma^te ys in better cace then they prowddist prynce of them all. . . . Here ys a Schote come from Diepe, whome was there as the xth of this present, whoe saythe that the Frenche King haythe no shipes in a redynes and a lacke both monny and men to put in them; and that now a haythe more nead to have men abowght hym sellfe for to deffend the great power that ys upe in France for to subdew Mon^sr do Guysse and his brethen.

❖

Index

Italic figures refer to plate numbers